R O B E R

GRANDPA

SAYS

LEAFWOOD
PUBLISHERS

A HERITAGE OF WISDOM
FOR THE NEXT GENERATION

Grandpa Says
A Heritage of Wisdom for the Next Generation

ISBN: 0-89112-514-0
Copyright © 2006 Leafwood Publishers
All rights reserved.
Printed in the U.S.A.
All scriptures, unless otherwise indicated, are taken from the Holy Bible, New
International Version® Copyright © 1973, 1978, 1984 by International Bible
Society. Used by permission of Zondervan Publishing House. All rights reserved.
Scripture quotations marked NLT are taken from the Holy Bible, New Living
Translation, copyright © 1996. Used by permission of Tyndale House Publishers,
Inc., Wheaton, Illinois 60189. All rights reserved.
Design by Greg Jackson, Thinkpen Design LLC, Springdale, AR
Any omission of credits is unintentional.

The publisher requests documentation for future printings.

Contents

TABLE OF CONTENTS

Dear Reader:

Today a great upheaval is taking place in our families, our culture, and our religious life in America and around the world. Right and wrong are being co-mingled in our culture every day. The strong ethical underpinnings of our society that made America great are being yanked from their moorings and are carelessly tossed to the wind. Our young people are not being taught by word and example fundamental moral values so desperately needed.

Grandpa Says addresses this situation. It is a collection of scriptures, quotes, sayings, and even humor on moral values that can help young people of today gain a solid footing on what is right and wrong. My hope and prayer is that by reading these pages and putting this advice into practice every day young people will grow up to be good parents, happy, productive citizens, and loving children of God.

Blessings as you read,

Robert J. Hall

"GRANDPA"

THEY CALL ME GRANDPA

Babies are such a
nice way to start people.

DON HERROLD

Blessed indeed is the man
who hears many gentle voices
call him father!

LYDIA M. CHILD

*When I first became a father, I was overwhelmed.
I couldn't believe how much responsibility I felt for that
helpless little baby. There was no instruction manual,
but somehow we—and our kids—survived! I'm convinced
there is no greater honor than being a father.
And now they call me Grandpa.*

ROBERT J. HALL

Sons are a heritage from the Lord,
children a reward from him.

PSALM 127:3

PROTECT YOUR FAMILY NAME

You have a good name. Honor it and keep it clean. In that way you
honor your mom and dad. Do nothing to tarnish your family name.

UNKNOWN

Whatever you do in life,
never do anything to embarrass the family name.

ANONYMOUS

A good name is seldom regained when character is gone.
One of the richest jewels of life is lost forever.

J. HANES

Have regard for your name since it will remain with you forever.

UNKNOWN

A good name is better than fine perfume.

ECCLESIASTES 7:1

A good name is more desirable than great riches;
to be esteemed is better than silver or gold.

PROVERBS 22:1

Remember that a man's name is, to him, the sweetest
and most important sound in any language.

DALE CARNEGIE

Your name
You got it from your father.
It was all he had to give.
So it's yours to use and cherish
For as long as you may live.
If you lose the watch he gave you
It can always be replaced.
But a black mark on your name, son
Can never be erased.
It was clean the day you took it
And a worthy name to bear.
When he got it from his father
There was no dishonor there.
So make sure you guard it wisely.
After all is said and done.
You'll be glad the name is spotless
When you give it to your son.

Lou Holtz, Head Coach, Notre Dame

An Indian petitioned a judge in a New Mexico court for
permission to change his name to a shorter one.
"What is your name now?" asked the judge.
"Chief Screeching Train Whistle."
"And what do you wish to change it to?"
The Indian folded his arms and grunted, "Toots."

Doc Blakely

HONESTY PAYS

Honesty is not the best policy—it is the only policy.

UNKNOWN

The Lord hates cheating and delights in honesty.

PROVERBS 11:1

In an honest transaction, both parties gain.

ROBERT P. VICHAS

Basic Operating Policy at Visador Company: Conduct business
affairs with truth, honesty and integrity.

ROBERT J. HALL

There is no right way to do something wrong.

UNKNOWN

The first step in greatness is to be honest.

SAMUEL JOHNSON

Honesty is the first chapter in the book of wisdom.

THOMAS JEFFERSON

I hope I shall possess firmness and virtue enough to maintain
what I consider the most enviable of all titles,
the character of an honest man.

GEORGE WASHINGTON

You can't go wrong by doing what's right.

COACH GENE STALLINGS

The late golf champion, Babe Didrikson Zaharias, once disqualified herself from a golf tournament for having hit the wrong ball out of the rough. "But nobody would have known," her friend told her. "I would have known," Babe Zaharias replied.

UNKNOWN

"Oh what a tangled web we weave
when first we practice to deceive."

WILLIAM SHAKESPEARE

Honesty is not only the best policy, it is the will of God.

GOD'S BEST FOR YOUR SUCCESS

One winter we broke the ice on an open pond to
baptize some people. "Is the water cold, Sam?"
asked a deacon of a shivering, dripping convert.
"No, not a bit cold," replied Sam.
"Better put him under again, parson," suggested the deacon,
"he hasn't quit lying yet."

LEROY BROWNLOW

What makes a person wise is understanding what to do.
But what makes a person foolish is dishonesty.

Foolish people don't care if they sin.
But honest people work at being right with others.

PROVERBS 14:8-9 ICB

Love is the Greatest Commandment

This is my commandment: Love each other.

JOHN 15:17

Love is patient, love is kind. It does not envy,
it does not boast, it is not proud. It is not rude, it is not self-
seeking, it is not easily angered, it keeps no record of wrongs.
Love does not delight in evil but rejoices with the truth. It always
protects, always trusts, always hopes, always perseveres.

I CORINTHIANS 13:4-7

Love people and use things. Don't love things and use people.

ART DeMOSS

The heart that loves is always young.

ANONYMOUS

God's love for us is not a love that always exempts us from trials,
but rather, a love that sees us through trials.

ELEANOR DOAN

Remember—"Jesus loves me, this I know."

The love of God is greater far than tongue or pen can ever tell.
F. M. LEHMAN

The entire law is summed up in a single command:
"Love your neighbor as yourself."
GALATIANS 5:14 NIV

To the loved a word of affection is a morsal,
but to the love-starved, a word of affection can be a feast.
MAX LUCADO

Love is what's left in a relationship
after all the selfishness has been removed.
CULLEN HIGHTOWER

Love doesn't make the world go round.
Love is what makes it worthwhile.
UNKNOWN

Love is the greatest of all words in our language.
COACH JOHN WOODEN

The preacher told the story in which he asked in a children's Bible
class, "If I should see a man beating a donkey and stopped him,
what virtue would I show?"
A little voice said, "Brotherly love."
LEROY BROWNLOW

OBEY AUTHORITY

We ought to obey God rather than men.

ACTS 5:29

The way a child sees his parents' leadership sets the tone
for his eventual relationships with his teachers, school principal,
police, neighbors, and employers. And ultimately, of course,
respect of earthly authority teaches children to yield to the
benevolent authority of God himself.

DR. JAMES DOBSON, DR. DOBSON ANSWERS YOUR QUESTIONS
ABOUT RAISING CHILDREN

Children, obey your parents in the Lord, for this is right.

EPHESIANS 6:1

A dying Christian father bade farewell to his family and then
turning to his wife said, "My dear, see that you bring the children
up to honor and obey you, for if they don't obey you when they are
young, they won't obey God when they are older."

HARRY A. IRONSIDE

Trust and obey, for there's no other way to be happy in Jesus,
but to trust and obey.

J. H. SAMMIS

Don't bite the hand that has your allowance in it.

CAROLYN COATS

The very idea of the power and right of the people
to establish government
presupposes the duty of every individual
to obey the established government.

GEORGE WASHINGTON

A child has to learn obedience in the home or he will never learn
obedience to the Heavenly Father.

DR. BOB SMITH

Proper authority is defined as loving leadership.
Without decision-makers and others who agree to follow,
there is inevitable chaos and confusion and disorder in human
relationships. Loving authority is absolutely necessary
for the healthy functioning family.

DR. JAMES DOBSON, DR. DOBSON ANSWERS YOUR QUESTIONS
ABOUT RAISING CHILDREN

If we are not governed by God, we will be ruled by tyrants.

WILLIAM PENN

When I was a kid, I was taught the laws of gravity—
shut up and sit down.

GARY APPLE

Wisdom Comes From God

For the Lord gives wisdom:
from his mouth comes knowledge and understanding.

PROVERBS 2:6

If any of you lack wisdom, he should ask God, who gives
generously to all without finding fault, and it will be given to him.

JAMES 1:5

Common sense, in an uncommon degree,
is what the world calls wisdom.

ELEANOR DOAN

The art of being wise is the art of knowing what to overlook.

CAROLYN COATS

One of life's mysteries is why we get old so soon...
and smart so late.

UNKNOWN

Don't overlook old people.
Here is wisdom and experience for our asking.
Here, also, is a group to whom we must give
kindness and affection.

DR. JOHN R. MOTT

A wise person considers the effects of a decision
on all involved, not just himself.

BOBB BIEHL

A smart man picks his friends wisely—not to pieces.

UNKNOWN

We quickly cease to make sense when we abandon the wisdom of
the Creator and substitute our own puny ideas of the moment.

DR. JAMES DOBSON, CHILDREN AT RISK

We can learn much from wise words,
little from wisecracks and less from wise guys.

WILLIAM ARTHUR WARD

A man should never be ashamed to say he has been wrong,
which is saying in other words that he is wiser today
than he was yesterday.

ALEXANDER POPE

Two men encounter a bear in the forest. One of the men pulls his
running shoes out of his knapsack and puts them on. The other
man says, incredulously, "You don't think that those running shoes
are going to help you outrun that bear?" The other man replies,
"I don't have to outrun the bear. I only have to outrun you!"

UNKNOWN

VALUES GUIDE YOU DAILY

Values are the right choices you must make in life
to put yourself in favor with God and man.

ROBERT J. HALL

The Boy Scouts of America teach great values in their Scout law:
A Scout is trustworthy, loyal, helpful, friendly, courteous, kind,
obedient, cheerful, thrifty, brave, clean and reverent.

Here is a simple, rule-of-thumb guide for behavior:
Ask yourself what you want people to do for you,
then grab the initiative and do it for them.
Add up God's Law and Prophets and this is what you get.

MATTHEW 7:12, THE MESSAGE

The basic principles laid down in the
Ten Commandments and the Sermon on the Mount
are as applicable today as when they were declared.

HERBERT HOOVER, AMERICAN PRESIDENT

Moderation in temper is always a virtue;
but moderation in principle is always a vice.

THOMAS PAINE 18TH-CENTURY ENGLISH ACTIVIST

"Grandpa Says..." is a book of values.
Make them a part of your everyday life.

ROBERT J. HALL

You can only achieve success and happiness
if your material goals are consistent with your core values.

SIR JOHN TEMPLETON

Those we choose as our associates will have
an impact on our values—for good or evil.

GOD'S BEST FOR YOUR SUCCESS

What shall it profit a man,
if he shall gain the whole world and lose his own soul.

MARK 8:36

If you are not doing what you value,
you don't value yourself.
Try not to become a man of success,
but rather try to become a man of value.

ALBERT EINSTEIN

To begin a discussion on values, our youth minister asked the
teens this question: "What would you do if your doctor told you
you had only twenty-four hours to live?" The teens' responses were
typically, "Be with friends and family." But the discussion came
undone when Jason, our thirteen-year-old, said,
"I'd get a second opinion."

DONNA SPRATT

Each of us possesses incredible value because we are
children of the Creator, who has a specific plan for our lives.

DR. JAMES DOBSON, HIDE OR SEEK

IF WE LOSE OUR VALUES, WE LOSE

The ultimate test of a civilization is not its power or its riches,
but its sense of values, and every flourishing empire of the past
collapsed because it began paying more attention to the
incidentals than to the essentials of a good life.

SYDNEY J. HARRIS

In this storm our children learned something.
They saw that a big man (Bill Clinton) did bad things,
and then they saw that even though he was very powerful,
the laws of the common people were still applied to him.
The crimes he committed were unearthed and investigated.
He was impeached in the House,
and his crimes were debated in the Senate.
It could not find the will to convict him,
but those senators who both were honest
and had a heart for what had happened in the country
stood up and called the big man's actions what they were,
low and cruel and wrong.

PEGGY NOONAN, THE WALL STREET JOURNAL

Blessed Lord, teach me your rules...
I will meditate upon them
and give them my full respect.
I will delight in them and not forget them.

PSALMS 119:12, 15-16 TLB

Whenever we build our lives on values
and principles that contradict the time-honored
wisdom of God's Word,
we are laying a foundation on the sand.

Dr. James Dobson

The best index to a person's character is
(a) how he treats people who can't do him any good and
(b) how he treats people who can't fight back.

Abigail Van Buren syndicated columnist

Kids want values,
but they are rightly suspicious of talk without action.
So while you need to talk to kids about values,
your words will be meaningless unless you live them as well.

Thomas E. Ricks, Parade Magazine

The Boy Scouts got it right with their Scout Oath:
On my honor I will do my best
To do my duty to God and my country
and to obey the Scout Law;
To help other people at all times;
To keep myself physically strong,
mentally awake, and morally straight.

Self-Discipline is Rewarded

Freedom without self-discipline is self-defeating.
ROBERT J. HALL

If any man will come after me, let him deny himself,
and take up his cross and follow me.
MATTHEW 16:24

Self-discipline is to remain always cool and
unruffled under all circumstances.
THOMAS JEFFERSON

Self-discipline is the hardest victory.
ARISTOTLE

A diplomat is a person who thinks twice before saying nothing.
CAROLYN COATS

Discipline is doing what doesn't come naturally.
UNKNOWN

People who fly into a rage often make a bad landing.
CAROLYN COATS

Hot heads and cold hearts never solved anything.
BILLY GRAHAM

What we do upon some great occasion will probably
depend on what we already are: and what we are will be
the result of previous years of self-discipline.

H. P. LIDDON

Life is a marathon, not a sprint.
It requires self-discipline and endurance.

GOD'S BEST FOR YOUR SUCCESS

The will is malleable. It can and should be molded and
polished—not to make a robot of a child for our selfish purposes,
but to give him the ability to control his own impulses, and
exercise self-discipline later in life.
In fact, we have a God-given responsibility to shape the will.

DR. JAMES DOBSON, THE STRONG-WILLED CHILD

Nothing is as hard to do gracefully as getting down
off your high horse.

CAROLYN COATS

Life is tons of discipline.

ROBERT FROST

He who reigns within himself, and rules passions,
desires, and fears, is more than a king.

JOHN MILTON

RESPONSIBILITY IS YOURS

Hold yourself responsible for a higher standard
than anybody else expects of you. Never excuse yourself.

HENRY WARD BEECHER

As human beings, we are endowed with freedom of choice,
and we cannot shuffle off our responsibility upon the shoulders of
God or nature. We must shoulder it ourselves. It is up to us.

ARNOLD J. TOYNBEE

The price of greatness is responsibility.

SIR WINSTON CHURCHILL

You can't escape the responsibility of tomorrow
by evading it today.

ABRAHAM LINCOLN

When I was a child I spoke and thought and reasoned
as a child does. But when I became a man my thoughts grew
far beyond those of my childhood,
and now I have put away the childish things.

I CORINTHIANS 13:11 TLB

My philosophy is that not only are you responsible for your life,
but doing the best at this moment
puts you in the best place for the next moment.

OPHRAH WINFREY

We should give conscious thought to the reasonable,
orderly transfer of freedom and responsibility,
so that we are preparing the child each year
for the moment of full independence which must come.

DR. JAMES DOBSON

The greatest gifts you can give your children are the roots of
responsibility and the wings of independence.

DENIS WAITLY

My parents, Buddy and Helen Watts, taught their children the
virtue of personal responsibility. Dad taught us, "When you make
a choice...good or bad...you and only you are responsible."
He would often say, "You buy your bed, you sleep in it."

J. C. WATTS, OKLAHOMA CONGRESSMAN

Be careful in life because you must
take responsibility for your own actions.

ROBERT J. HALL

A youth answered an advertisement for a responsible boy. "What
makes you think you're responsible?" asked the employer. "On
every job I have ever had so far," the young man answered,
"whenever anything went wrong, the boss has always said to me,
'You're responsible!' "

UNKNOWN

BE A PERSON OF INTEGRITY

Your word is your bond—keep it.

UNKNOWN

The key question you must always ask yourself:
"What is the right thing to do?"

UNKNOWN

A person is not given integrity. It results from
the relentless pursuit of honesty at all times.

UNKNOWN

The bottom line—do what is legal, fair and right.

ROBERT J. HALL

Integrity is the glue that holds our way of life together.

BILLY GRAHAM

The supreme quality for a leader is unquestionably integrity.
Without it, no real success is possible, no matter whether it is on a
section gang, a football field, in an army or in an office.

DWIGHT D. EISENHOWER

When no one is watching, live as if someone is.

MAX LUCADO

Sheer ability is not enough to succeed in life, at least not for the long haul. Personal integrity is basic to long-term success.

GOD'S BEST FOR YOUR SUCCESS

So he shepherded them according to the integrity of his heart, and guided them by the skillfulness of his hands.

PSALM 78:72

The ultimate measure of man is not where he stands in moments of comfort and convenience, but where he stands at times of challenge and controversy.

MARTIN LUTHER KING, JR.

Lessons of Integrity learned by Marine recruits at Parris Island:

Tell the truth

Do your best, no matter how trivial the task.

Choose the difficult right over the easy wrong.

Look out for the group before you look out for yourself.

Don't whine or make excuses.

Judge others by their actions not their race.

THOMAS E. RICKS

With integrity you won't be afraid to sell the family parrot to the town gossip.

WILL ROGERS

Establish Goals

Life without goals is like a race without a finish line.
ED TRENNER

Knowing what our goal is and desiring to reach it
doesn't bring us closer to it. Doing something does.
ELEANOR L. DOAN

Education teaches a student good marksmanship
before he takes aim at his goal in life.
UNKNOWN

Set your goals high. You may not reach it,
but you'll put on muscle climbing toward it.
UNKNOWN

The first two letters of the word goal spell go.
ELEANOR L. DOAN

Set goals. If you don't set goals,
you can't regret not reaching them.
YOGI BERRA

People with goals succeed because they know where they're going.
EARL NIGHTINGALE

If a man knows not what harbor he seeks,
any wind is the right wind.

SENECA

The most important thing about goals is having one.

GEOFFRY F. ABERT

A man without a purpose is like a ship without a rudder.

THOMAS CARLYLE

Achieving well-selected goals is but a stepping stone
to bigger and better things.

ROBERT J. HALL

King Solomon gave us the most important of all life's goals:
Now all has been heard; here is the conclusion of the
matter: Fear God and keep his commandments, for
this is the whole duty of man.

ECCLESIASTES 12:13

The goal I believe is important is the goal of making the most of
your abilities. That goal is within your reach. If pursuing material
things becomes your only goal, you will fail in so many other ways.
Besides, in time all material things go away.

COACH JOHN WOODEN

Men, like tacks, are useful if they have good heads
and are pointed in the right direction.

SPEAKER'S SOURCEBOOK

Be Courteous At All Times

When visiting away from home, eat what you are fed,
sleep where you're put, and always say, "Thank you."
EVIDA BIEHL

Nothing costs so little and goes so far as courtesy.
UNKNOWN

Life is not so short but that there is always time for courtesy.
RALPH WALDO EMERSON

Proper courtesy should be observed even between close friends.
JAPANESE PROVERB

When you are courteous to others
you show dignity and respect to them.
ROBERT J. HALL

There is no outward sign of true courtesy that does not rest
on a deep moral foundation.
JOHANN VON GOETHE

Honor your father and mother.
EPHESIANS 6:2

The grace of God is courtesy.
HILAIRE BELLOC

Finally, all of you, live in harmony with one another; be
sympathetic, love as brothers, be compassionate and humble.

I Peter 3:8

Being polite and courteous isn't paying a price any more than
smiling or being happy is paying a price.
You get more than you give when you are polite and courteous.
You don't pay. You are paid.

Coach John Wooden

Good manners are like traffic rules for society.

Michael Levine, Lessons at the Halfway Point

Once at the grocery store this lady couldn't park her car because
there was a cart in the way so I moved it so she could park her car
and she thanked me for doing that.

Rachel, 5th grade

A young lad had returned from a birthday party.
His mother, apprehensive lest his appetite should have
overcome his manners, asked,
"Are you sure you didn't ask your hostess
for a second piece of cake?"
"Oh, no, mother. I only asked her for the recipe so you could bake
a cake like it, and she insisted on giving me two more pieces.

Braude's Handbook of Humor

SHAME HURTS

Shame is a painful sense of guilt
arising from acting in a dishonorable way.

S. I. HAYAKAWA

Whether public or private, shame is always painful.
Unless you deal with it, it is permanent.

MAX LUCADO

Shame like pain is God's way of telling us
we are harming ourselves.

ROBERT J. HALL

I regard that man as lost, who has lost his sense of shame.

PLAUTUS

He who ignores discipline comes to poverty and shame,
but whoever heeds correction is honored.

PROVERBS 13:18

We are young only once, but we can be immature indefinitely.

CAROLYN COATS

Shame induces us to fear sin.

HEBREW PROVERB

Shame sometimes can kill a man.

PHILIPPINE PROVERB

Those who look to Him (the Lord) are radiant;
their faces are never covered with shame.

PSALMS 34:5

You can't act like a skunk without someone's getting wind of it.

UNKNOWN

When wickedness comes, so does contempt,
and with shame comes disgrace.

PROVERBS 18:3

Where there's no shame before men, there's no fear of God.

YIDDISH PROVERB

If anyone is ashamed of me and my words in this adulterous
and sinful generation, the Son of Man will be ashamed of him
when he comes in his Father's glory with the holy angels.

MARK 8:38

Lady to Beggar: "Aren't you ashamed of yourself to stand here
begging on the street?"

Beggar: "What do you want, lady; should I open an office?"

UNKNOWN

SHARE WITH OTHERS

I believe the greatest joy one can have is doing something for
someone else without any thought of getting something in return.

COACH JOHN WOODEN

The fragrance always remains in the hand that gives the rose.

HEDA BEJAR

It is more blessed to give than to receive.

ACTS 20:35

You can hardly become greedy or selfish
when you are busily sharing what you have with others.

DR. JAMES DOBSON, LOVE FOR A LIFETIME

There is a wonderful, almost mystical, law of nature that says
three of the things we want most—happiness, freedom, and peace
of mind—are always attained when we give them to others.

COACH JOHN WOODEN

Don't give till it hurts: Give a little more . . . give till it feels good.

ELEANOR DOAN

The first great gift we can bestow on others is a good example.

THOMAS MORELL

A giving attitude is the secret to successful living.

ROBERT H. SCHULLER

He who gives quickly gives doubly.

GERMAN PROVERB

The way we clutch our possessions and our pennies,
you'd think we couldn't live without them.

MAX LUCADO

Just as Canadian geese share in leading the flock
as they wing their way south for the winter, so, too, must we share
our abilities with others to reach our common goals.

ROBERT J. HALL

God does not charge time spent helping others
against a person's allotted time span.

AMERICAN INDIAN PROVERB

Teacher: "If your mother gave you a large apple and a small apple
and told you to divide with your brother,
which would you give him?"
Tommy: "Do you mean my little brother or my big brother?"

BRAUDE'S HANDBOOK OF HUMOR

USE TIME WISELY

Every time the clock ticks, you have one second less to finish the job
you are doing and one second less to attain the goals in your life.

BRIAN TRACY

If you do not have the time to do it right,
when will you find the time to do it over?

COACH JOHN WOODEN

Time has a way of separating wants from needs.

MAX LUCADO

I have a right to use or even waste my time if I choose,
but I have no right to waste your time.

ROBERT J. HALL

Time once lost is gone forever.

ELEANOR DOAN

Mastering your time is mastering your life.

BRIAN TRACY

Time and tide wait for no man.

ENGLISH PROVERB

Remember the rule—Be on time for Sunday School.

ESTELLE ROBINSON

Nothing valuable can be lost by taking time.

ABRAHAM LINCOLN

The first and most important step in improving
the use of our time is planning.

ANONYMOUS

There is a time for everything,
and a season for every activity under heaven:

a time to be born and a time to die,
a time to plant and a time to uproot,
a time to kill and a time to heal,
a time to tear down and a time to build,
a time to weep and a time to laugh,
a time to mourn and a time to dance,
a time to scatter stones and a time to gather them,
a time to embrace and a time to refrain,
a time to search and a time to give up,
a time to keep and a time to throw away,
a time to tear and a time to mend,
a time to be silent and a time to speak,
a time to love and a time to hate,
a time for war and a time for peace.

ECCLESIASTES 3:1-8

CONTROL YOUR TONGUE

Handle words carefully,
for they have more power than atomic bombs.

PEARL STRACHAN HURD

When you are offered a morsel of gossip marinated in slander,
do you turn it down or pass it on?

MAX LUCADO

Usually the first screw that gets loose in a person's head
is the one that controls the tongue.

ELEANOR DOAN

Teach your child to hold his tongue,
he'll learn fast enough to speak.

BENJAMIN FRANKLIN

A sharper weapon than the sword.

PHOCYLIDES

A soft answer turns away wrath, but harsh words cause quarrels.

PROVERBS 15:1 TLB

A man of knowledge uses words with restraint,
and a man of understanding is even-tempered.

PROVERBS 17:27

A fool's tongue is long enough to cut his own throat.

ENGLISH PROVERB

Real friends warm you with their presence, trust you with their
secrets and remember you with their prayers.

SPIRITUAL REFLECTIONS

Promise to give so much time to improving yourself
that you have no time to criticize others.

COACH JOHN WOODEN

Often the best thing about not saying anything
is that it can't be repeated.

SUZAN L. WIENER

Never miss a chance to keep your mouth shut.

ROBERT NEWTON PECK, A DAY NO PIGS WOULD DIE

The magician's hand may be quicker than the eye
but the scandal-monger's tongue is quicker than lightning.

B. M. STANSIFER

He who thinks by the inch, and talks by the yard...
should be kicked by the foot.

DOC BLAKELY

"By swallowing evil words unsaid,
no one has ever harmed his stomach."

WINSTON CHURCHILL

KINDNESS ENRICHES

Kindness is purely and simply being willing to do what is obvious
and necessary at any given moment—
simply a matter of treating everyone as though they were
a brother or sister who happens to be in need.

UNKNOWN

Never lose a chance of saying a kind word.

WILLIAM MAKEPEACE THACKERAY

[5]For this very reason, make every effort to add to
your faith goodness; and to goodness, knowledge; [6]and to
knowledge, self-control; and to self-control, perseverance; and to
perseverance, godliness; [7]and to godliness, brotherly kindness;
and to brotherly kindness, love.

2 PETER 1:5-7 NIV

Treat people like angels; you will meet some and help make some.

MAX LUCADO

Speak kinds words and you will hear kind echoes.

UNKNOWN

Kindness enriches others, rewards the giver, and honors God.

ROBERT J. HALL

Wise sayings often fall on barren ground;
but a kind word is never thrown away.

SIR ARTHUR HELPS

To me a random act of kindness means in your own special
way doing something that makes the world a better place.
I think if everyone would commit themselves to doing
a kind act the world would run a little smoother.

GEORGE, 6TH GRADE

If you were paid ten cents for every kind word you ever spoke,
and had to pay out five cents for every unkind word,
would you be rich or poor?

UNKNOWN

Never let an opportunity pass to say a kind and encouraging
word to or about somebody. Praise good work.

UNKNOWN

The way to make yourself pleasing to others is to show that you care
for them...The seeds of love can never grow but under the warm and
genial influence of kind feelings and affectionate manners.

WILLIAM WIRT TO HIS DAUGHTER

Patient: "How can I ever repay you for your kindness to me?"

Doctor: "By check, money order, or cash."

BRAUDE'S HANDBOOK OF HUMOR

BE A DOER

Do what you can, with what you have, where you are.

THEODORE ROOSEVELT

It's important to keep trying to do what you think is right
no matter how hard it is or how often you fail.
You never stop trying. I'm still trying.

COACH JOHN WOODEN

I have learned the secret of being content
in any and every situation...
I can do everything through him who gives me strength.

PHILLIPIANS 4:12-13 NIV

Nothing results from apathy.

MAX LUCADO

Don't just stand there. Do something,
even if it is wrong. If it's wrong, then fix it.

J. D. HALL, JR.

Yes, haste makes waste, but indecision is just as bad.
Strike a balance but do something.

ROBERT J. HALL

To love someone more dearly every day,
to help a wandering child to find his way,
to ponder o'er a noble thought and pray,
and smile when evening falls: this is my task.

MAUDE LOUISE RAY (1903)

The true calling of a Christian is not to do extraordinary things
but to do ordinary things in an extraordinary way.

DEAN STANLEY

Better to do something imperfectly than to do nothing flawlessly .

ROBERT H. SCHULLER

Doing nothing is tiresome—you can't stop and rest.

CAROLYN COATS

At Christmas time, get a group of friends together
and sing carols at a local hospital.

UNKNOWN

Iron rusts from disuse, stagnant water loses its purity
and in cold weather becomes frozen;
even so does inaction sap the vigors of the mind.

LEONARDO DA VINCI (1452-1519)

Words are plentiful, but deeds are precious.

LECH WALESA

FRIENDS HELP FRIENDS

You can make more friends in two months by
becoming interested in other people than you can in
two years by trying to get other people interested in you.

DALE CARNEGIE

True friends are those who, when you've made a fool of yourself,
don't think you've done a permanent job.

UNKNOWN

The only safe and sure way to destroy an enemy
is to make him your friend.

UNKNOWN

Greater love has no one than this,
that he lay down his life for his friends.

JOHN 15:13 NIV

Friendships cemented together with sin do not hold.

UNKNOWN

If a man does not make new acquaintances
as he passes through life, he will soon find himself left alone.
A man should keep his friendships in constant repair.

JOHNSON

True friendship is like sound health,
the value of it is seldom known until it be lost.

Charles Caleb Colton (1780-1832)

Sacred delight is having God as your pinch-hitter, your lawyer,
your dad, your biggest fan, and your best friend.

Max Lucado

A friend is not so much one to whom you can go for help when you
are in trouble...That has its value, but a friend is one to whom you
can go when HE is in trouble!

Unknown

Love is much too pure and holy,
friendship is too sacred far,
for a moment's reckless folly
thus to desolate and mar.

Sunday School teacher (1867)

The happiest miser on Earth...
is the man who saves every friend he can make.

Unknown

My wife and I received a note the other day from an
8-year old friend. The neatly penned message: "Thank you
for coming to my party. Thank you for my present.
I have to go to the bathroom now, so goodbye."

Doc Blakely

LIFE CAN BE TOUGH

Tough times never last, but tough people do.

ROBERT H. SCHULLER

Life is a trial, mile by mile. Life is hard, yard by yard.
But it's a cinch, inch by inch.

UNKNOWN

Live every day as if it were your last.
Do every job as if you were the boss.
Drive as if all other vehicles were police cars.
Treat everybody else as if he were you.

PHOENIX FLAME

I am the way, the truth, and the life:
no man cometh unto the Father, but by me.

JOHN 14:6

When upon life's billows you are tempest tossed,
when you are discouraged, thinking all is lost,
count your many blessings, name them one by one,
and it will surprise you what the Lord hath done.

JOHNSON OATMAN

It takes both rain and sunshine to make a rainbow.

UNKNOWN

Life is a journey in which one makes a choice of
where he will spend eternity—either Heaven or Hell.

ROBERT J. HALL

The rule that governs my life is this: Anything that dims
my vision of Christ, or takes away my taste for Bible study, or
cramps my prayer life, or makes Christian work difficult, is wrong
for me, and I must, as a Christian, turn away from it.

J. WILBUR CHAPMAN

Life, like a mirror, never gives back more than we put into it.

UNKNOWN

The law of worthy life is essentially the law of strife.
It is only through labor and painful effort, by grim energy
and resolute courage that we move on to better things.

THEODORE ROOSEVELT

Let God have your life; He can do more with it than you can.

D. L. MOODY

A nervous passenger on an elevator asked the operator,
"What would happen if the cable broke?
Would we go up or down?"
The exasperated operator replied,
"That, madam, depends on the life you've led."

DOC BLAKELY

Character is Priceless

Character is what you really are;
reputation is merely what you are perceived to be.

COACH JOHN WOODEN

A good name is seldom regained. When character is gone,
one of the richest jewels of life is lost forever.

J. HANES

When wealth is lost, nothing is lost; when health is lost,
something is lost; when character is lost, all is lost!

MOTTO OVER THE WALLS OF A SCHOOL IN GERMANY

A wife of noble character, who can find?
She is worth far more than rubies...
her children arise and call her blessed;
her husband also, and he praises her.

PROVERBS 31:10,28 NIV

A man's character is like a fence—
it cannot be strengthened by whitewash.

UNKNOWN

Do not be misled; bad company corrupts good character.

I CORINTHIANS 15:33 NIV

I'd rather see a sermon, than hear one any day.
I'd rather walk with men of character and honor
and watch them lead the way.
For the best of all men are the men who live their creeds.
To see good works in action is what this nation needs.
The sound advice you give me may be very good and true;
But, I'd rather learn my lessons by observing what you do.
I may misunderstand you and the wise advice you give;
But there is no misunderstanding observing how you act and live.

WILLIAM A. CARPENTER

Truthfulness is a corner-stone in character,
and if it be not firmly laid in youth,
there will ever after be a weak spot in the foundation.

JEFFERSON DAVIS

Leadership is a potent combination of strategy and character. But
if you must be without one, be without the strategy.

GEN. H. NORMAN SCHWARZKOPF

When my great-niece was 5, she asked her grandmother,
"Grandma, are you rotten on the inside?"

"No, sweetheart, why?" Grandma answered with some surprise.
"Because when apples are all wrinkled on the outside,

they are rotten on the inside."

SHERMALEE OCHOA

GOD'S TOUCH MAKES YOU SPECIAL

The Touch of the Master's Hand
It was battered and scarred, and the auctioneer
Thought it scarcely worth the while,
To waste much time on the old violin,
But he held it up with a smile.

"What am I bid for this old violin?
Who will start the bidding for me?
A dollar, a dollar, who'll make it two?
Two dollars, and who'll make it three?"

"Three dollars once, three dollars twice,
Going for three," but no;
From the back of the room a gray haired man
Came forward and took up the bow.

Then wiping the dust from the old violin,
And tightening up all the strings,
He played a melody pure and sweet,
As sweet as the angels sing.

The music ceased and the auctioneer
With a voice that was quiet and low
Said, "What am I bid for the old violin?"
And he held it up with the bow.

"A thousand dollars, and who'll make it two?
Two thousand, and who'll make it three?
Three thousand once, three thousand twice,
Going, and gone," said he.

The people cheered, but some of them said,
"We do not quite understand,
What changed its worth?" Came the reply,
"The touch of the master's hand."

And many a man with his life out of tune,
And battered and scarred with sin,
Is auctioned cheap to a thoughtless crowd,
Much like the old violin.

A mess of pottage, a glass of wine,
A game, and he shuffles along.
He's going once, and he's going twice,
He's going and almost gone.

But the Master comes, and the thoughtless crowd
Never can quite understand
The worth of the soul, and the change that is wrought
By the touch of the Master's hand.

Myra Brooks Welch

Draw nearer to God, and he will draw near to you.

James 4:8

WINNERS LISTEN

A good listener is not only popular everywhere,
but after a while he knows something.

WILSON MIZNER

My dear brothers, take note of this: Everyone should be quick to
listen, slow to speak and slow to become angry.

JAMES 1:19 NIV

Listen to those under your supervision. Really listen. Don't act as
though you're listening and let it go in one ear and out the other.
Faking it is worse than not doing it at all.

COACH JOHN WOODEN

The mark of a disciple is his or her ability
to hear the Master's voice.

MAX LUCADO

Most of the successful people I've known are ones who do more
listening than talking. If you choose your company carefully,
it's worth listening to what they have to say. You don't have to
blow out the other fellow's light to let your own shine.

BERNARD BARUCH

There's no one as deaf as he who will not listen.

YIDDISH

The good Lord may have made a suggestion as to
how much we should talk vs. how much we should listen—
He gave us only one mouth, but two ears.

Robert J. Hall

Man's ears are not made to shut, but his mouth is.

Unknown

One thing you must not listen to is gossip.

Robert J. Hall

A pair of good ears will drink dry a hundred tongues.

Benjamin Franklin

If you want your wife to listen, talk to another woman.

Unknown

Four-year-old Jason was visiting his grandparents.
Grandpa was in his study intently reading. Jason walked in
carrying a peach, said something Grandpa didn't catch,
and handed the peach to him.

Thinking his wife had sent him a snack, Grandpa took it
and ate it. Just as he swallowed the last bite, Jason, with lip
quivering, said, "But, Pap, I didn't want you to eat it.
I just wanted you to get the worm out!"

Sue Hammons

Don't Carry Grudges

Grudge is one of those words that defines itself.
Its very sound betrays its meaning.

MAX LUCADO

You shall not take vengeance,
nor bear any grudge against the children of your people,
but you shall love your neighbor as yourself: I am the Lord.

LEVITICUS 19:18

Don't bear a grudge and don't record it.

JAPANESE PROVERB

If people walk all over you have you considered a linoleum vest?

ROBERT ORBEN

I shall allow no man to belittle my soul by making me hate him.

BOOKER T. WASHINGTON

Wanted: A boy who neither bullies other boys nor allows other
boys to bully him.

FRANK CRANE

Grudges love freshly gathered insults, whether real or imagined.

MARK FROST

Congratulations! You have been wronged, hurt, offended. You
are now the proud owner of a grudge. If properly cared for, your
grudge will give you a lifetime of companionship.

MARK FROST

A grudge, slander, and a chip on the shoulder
all have the same father—vengeance.

ROBERT J. HALL

An act of justice closes the book on a misdeed;
an act of vengeance writes one of its own.

MARILYN VOS SAVANT

Bitterness and resentment are emotional cancers
that rot us from within.

DR. JAMES DOBSON, DR. DOBSON ANSWERS YOUR QUESTIONS
ABOUT CONFIDENT, HEALTHY FAMILIES

Time spent getting even would be better spent trying to get ahead.

COACH JOHN WOODEN

The man who can smile when things go wrong
has thought of someone else he can blame it on.

DOC BLAKELY

FORGIVE TO BE FORGIVEN

Never does the human soul appear so strong and noble
as when it foregoes revenge, and dares to forgive an injury.

EDWIN HUBBELL CHAPIN

Bear with each other and forgive whatever grievances
you may have against one another. Forgive as the Lord
forgave you. And over all these virtues put on love,
which binds them all together in perfect unity.

COLOSSIANS 3:13-14

Forgive and forget. When you bury a mad dog,
don't leave his tail above the ground.

CHARLES SPURGEON

Every person should have a special cemetery lot
in which to bury the faults of friends and loved ones.

ANONYMOUS

The American people are very generous people and will forgive
almost any weakness, with the possible exception of stupidity.

WILL ROGERS

Forgiveness blesses all: the one who forgives;
the forgiven; and their mutual friends.

ROBERT J. HALL

There are times when we are called to love, expecting nothing in return. . .when we are called to give money to people who will never say thanks, to forgive those who won't forgive us.

MAX LUCADO

For if you forgive men when they sin against you, your heavenly Father will also forgive you. But if you do not forgive men their sins, your Father will not forgive your sins.

MATTHEW 6:14-15

Doing an injury puts you below your enemy; Revenging one makes you but even with him; Forgiving it sets you above him.

BENJAMIN FRANKLIN

Get rid of all bitterness, rage and anger, brawling and slander, along with every form of malice.
Be kind and compassionate to one another, forgiving each other, just as in Christ God forgave you.

EPHESIANS 4:31-32

No one said forgiveness is easy. The Bible is filled with exhortations to love your enemies. "Forgive us our trespasses, as we forgive those who trespass against us," says the Lord's Prayer.

THE ASSOCIATED PRESS

A small boy, repeating the Lord's Prayer one evening prayed: "And forgive us our debts as we forgive those who are dead against us."

ANONYMOUS

God Made America Great

I sought for the key to the greatness and genius of
America in her harbors...; in her fertile fields and boundless
forests; in her rich mines and vast world commerce; in her public
school system and institutions of learning. I sought for it in her
democratic Congress and in her matchless Constitution.

Not until I went into the churches of America
and heard her pulpits flame with righteousness did I
understand the secret of her genius and power.

ALEXIS DE TOCQUEVILLE

Righteousness exalts a nation, but sin is a disgrace to any people.

PROVERBS 14:34

Our country, right or wrong.
When right, to be kept right; when wrong, to be put right.

CARL SCHURZ, SOCIAL ACTIVIST, 1899

I see America, not in the setting sun of a black night of despair
ahead of us, I see America in the crimson light of a rising sun fresh
from the burning, creative hand of God. I see great days ahead,
great days possible to men and women of will and vision.

CARL SANDBURG

The fear of the Lord is the beginning of wisdom.

ABRAHAM LINCOLN

Americans shouldn't have to go to war every morning for their values. They already go to work for their families. They fight to hold down a job, raise responsible kids, make their payments, keep gas in the car, put food on the table and clothes on their backs, and still save a little to live their final days in dignity.

CHARLTON HESTON

What people want is very simple.
They want an America as good as its promise.

BARBARA JORDAN, FORMER CONGRESSWOMAN

America is great because America is good, and if America ever ceases to be good, America will cease to be great.

ALEXIS DE TOCQUEVILLE

Today, more than ever before Americans must stand up
for their rights as a God-fearing people.

ROBERT J. HALL

A Bible and a newspaper in every house, a good school in every district—all studied and appreciated as they merit—are the principal support of virtue, morality, and civil liberty.

BENJAMIN FRANKLIN

I pledge allegiance to the flag of the United States of America and to the Republic for which it stands, one nation under God, indivisible, with liberty and justice for all.

SERVE OTHERS

The service we render to others is really
the rent we pay for our room on this earth.

SIR WILFRED T. GRENFELL

It is one of the most beautiful compensations of this life that no
man can sincerely help another without helping himself.

RALPH WALDO EMERSON

Whoever wants to become great among you must be your servant,
and whoever wants to be first must be your slave—
just as the Son of Man did not come to be served, but to serve,
and to give his life as a ransom for many.

MATTHEW 20:26-28

Do not wait for leaders; do it alone, person to person.

MOTHER TERESA

There is a wonderful, almost mystical, law of nature that says
three of the things we want most—happiness, freedom, and peace
of mind—are always attained when we give them to others.

COACH JOHN WOODEN

The only ones among you who will be really happy
are those who will have sought and found how to serve.

ALBERT SCHWEITZER

A servant should be like a ticking clock:

Quietly going about his business,—
being helpful to others,—
always being on time.

ROBERT J. HALL

No one can serve two masters. Either he will hate the one and love the other, or he will be devoted to the one and despise the other.

MATTHEW 6:24

The image of George Washington kneeling in prayer at Valley Forge says something about the method of all leadership—humble, modest service.

GEORGE SWEETING

Service is love in work clothes.

UNKNOWN

The motorist had just bought a tankful of gasoline, and the station attendant was going through his little ritual.

Attendant: "Check your oil, sir?"
Motorist: "No, it's O.K."
Attendant: "Got enough water in your radiator?"
Motorist: "Yes, filled up."
Attendant: "Anything else, sir?"
Motorist: "Yes, would you please stick out your tongue so I can seal this letter?"

THE PUBLIC SPEAKER'S TREASURE CHEST

GENTLENESS MAKES YOU STRONG

Nothing is so strong as gentleness;
nothing so gentle as real strength.

FRANCIS OF SALES

But you, man of God, flee from all this, and pursue righteousness,
godliness, faith, love, endurance and gentleness.

I TIMOTHY 6:11

It took me a long time to understand
that even a stubborn mule responds to gentleness.

COACH JOHN WOODEN

Gentle words can overcome the harsh,
nasty tongue of an adversary.

ROBERT J. HALL

Criticism, like rain, should be gentle enough to nourish one's
growth without destroying one's roots.

BITS & PIECES

When we speak kindly, we recall that this is who we truly are,
a person of gentleness and warmth.

UNKNOWN

I would say to all: use your gentlest voice at home.

UNKNOWN

Gentleness is everywhere in daily life,
a sign that faith rules through ordinary things...
Even in a time of elephantine vanity and greed,
one never has to look far to see the campfires of gentle people.

GARRISON KEILLOR

We are indebted to Christianity for gentleness,
especially toward women.

CHARLES SIMMONS

Gentle lights: A businessman choosing honesty.
A hospital choosing compassion. A celebrity choosing kindness.
Visible evidence of the invisible hand.

MAX LUCADO

Paul asked his cousin, "What's the best way to teach a girl to
swim?" "That's a job that takes great skill," answered his cousin,
Bill. "You must be gentle and kind with her, having her walk out to
water that's about waist-deep. Then you put your arm around
her waist, gently encouraging her to lie down across it.
With your other hand, you pull her ankles up onto the surface of
the water, working her legs in a kicking motion. . ."

"It's my sister," interrupted Paul.
"Oh," answered Bill. "In that case, just push her off the dock."

DOC BLAKELY

BE HAPPY!

Most people are about as happy
as they make up their minds to be.

ABRAHAM LINCOLN

Many persons have a wrong idea about what
constitutes true happiness. It is not attained through
self-gratification, but through fidelity to a worthy purpose.

HELEN KELLER

But may the righteous be glad and rejoice before God;
may they be happy and joyful.

PSALMS 68:3

Happiness is different from pleasure. Happiness has something to
do with struggling and enduring and accomplishing.

GEORGE SHEEHAN

Sharing in the happiness of others is actually an act of kindness to
ourselves—we affirm our belief in the limitlessness of happiness.

UNKNOWN

Happiness it seems, has no logic.
It is not to be found in the facts of our lives, but rather in the
thoughts we entertain relative to those facts.

LEROY BROWNLOW

You will be happy when you make others happy.

ROBERT J. HALL

Happiness is inward and not outward;
and so it does not depend on what we have, but on what we are.

HENRY VAN DYKE

Is any one of you in trouble? He should pray.
Is anyone happy? Let him sing songs of praise.

JAMES 5:13

Sing and be happy, press on to the goal, trust Him who leads you,
He will keep your soul; let all be faithful, look to Him and pray,
lift your voice and praise Him in song, sing and be happy today.

EMORY S. PECK (1940)

Happiness is a perfume you can't pour on others
without getting a few drops on yourself.

UNKNOWN

A long married couple was sitting in the living room. He was
asleep in his easy chair and she was watching television. Suddenly,
a violent tornado struck the house. It ripped off the roof, picked
the man and woman up, swirled them into the air, and deposited
them a mile from home. The husband, seeing his wife sobbing,
said, "Stop crying, can't you see we're safe?" She whimpered, "I'm
just crying because I'm so happy. This is the first time we have
been out together in ten years."

DOC BLAKELY

PERSISTENCE DOESN'T QUIT

Persistence: The power to hold on in spite of everything, the
power to endure—this is the winner's quality. Persistence means
taking pains to overcome every obstacle, and to do what's
necessary to reach our goals. Sir Winston Churchill's whole speech
to a Cambridge University graduating class was—
"Never, never, never, never, never give up."

UNKNOWN

Great works are performed not by strength, but by perseverance.

SAMUEL JOHNSON

Many years ago, an entrepreneur had a very big dream.
He needed capital. He went to 301 banks,
and 301 banks said "no" to his dream. Then the 302nd bank said,
"OK, we'll help you build your theme park, Mr. Disney."

UNKNOWN

Don't quit. For if you do, you may miss the answer to your prayers.

MAX LUCADO

The only way to make a "come back" is to go on.

UNKNOWN

Persistence is stubbornness with a purpose.

R ICHARD D E V OS , C O - F OUNDER , A MWAY

Blessed is the man who perseveres under trial,
because when he has stood the test, he will receive the crown of
life that God has promised to those who love him.

J AMES 1:12

Nothing in the world can take the place of persistence.
Talent will not; nothing is more common than unsuccessful
men with talent. Genius will not; unrewarded genius is almost a
proverb. Education will not; the world is full of educated derelicts.
Persistence and determination alone are omnipotent.

C ALVIN C OOLIDGE

Through the troubled waters of life one must persevere
with each stroke of the oars to reach the far shore.

R OBERT J .H ALL

Teacher (lecturing on perseverance): "He drove straight
to his goal. He looked neither to the right nor to the left, but pressed
forward, moved by a definite purpose. Neither friend nor foe could
delay him, nor turn him from his course. All who crossed his path
did so at their own peril. What would you call such a man?

Graduate: "A truck driver!"

U NKNOWN

EARTHLY POSSESSIONS
ARE JUST THINGS

The most important things in life aren't things.

CAROLYN COATS

I am inclined to feel that our society as a whole has become
so infatuated with material things that we have gotten away from
the fundamental values and ideals. We seek happiness in the
wrong places and in the wrong form. Now parents will say, "We're
just trying to make ends meet," and they're telling the truth.
But if you think too much about the pursuit of material things,
you're going to hurt those youngsters you're working
so hard to buy material things for.

COACH JOHN WOODEN

But godliness with contentment is great gain. For we brought
nothing into the world, and we can take nothing out of it. But if
we have food and clothing, we will be content with that. People
who want to get rich fall into temptation and a trap and into many
foolish and harmful desires that plunge men into ruin and
destruction. For the love of money is a root of all kinds of evil.

I TIMOTHY 6:6-10

Would you really rather have a few possessions on earth
than eternal possessions in heaven?

MAX LUCADO

Earthly things are nice but they won't help you get to heaven.

ROBERT J. HALL

As former President George Bush said in his inaugural address,
"We are not the sum of our possessions."

GEORGE BUSH

It's good to have money and the things that money can buy,
but it's good, too, to check up once in a while and make
sure you haven't lost the things that money can't buy.

G. H. LARIMER

When a man gets rich, God gets a partner,
or the man loses his soul.

UNKNOWN

King Solomon instructs all: "Vanity of vanities," says the Preacher,
"All is vanity." Let us hear the conclusion of the whole matter: Fear
God and keep His commandments, for this is the whole duty of man.

ECCLESIASTES 12:8,13

The preacher received a letter from a private college
offering him an honorary doctor's degree.

In his answer he said, "I quickly accept. My only request is that
you hurry it up before you learn the rumor is not true:
I did not inherit all that money."

LEROY BROWNLOW

WORDS OF GOOD ADVICE

Here are ten wise rules from a famous grandfather.

1. Begin the day with cleanliness. Keep your bathroom immaculate.
2. Before leaving your room in the morning put all dis-carded clothing into a dresser or a closet.
3. Dress yourself neatly; other people can judge us only by what they see, until they know us well; and their judgments will affect our progress and our happiness.
4. Enter into the life of the family and the community with good cheer; make little of your troubles, much of your good fortune.
5. Do not speak while another is speaking. Discuss, do not dispute. Absorb and acknowledge whatever truth you can find in opinions different from your own.
6. Be courteous and considerate to all, especially to those who oppose you.
7. Reduce to a minimum your reading, hearing, and watching of material intended for immature minds. The mind is formed by what it takes in. Don't be a waste-basket.
8. Do some studying every day; grow old learning.
9. Combine external modesty with internal pride. Your modesty will make it easier for those around you to bear with you; your internal pride will stir you to shun meanness and sloth.
10. You will find in the Golden Rule the simplest and surest secret of happiness.

WILL DURANT, PHILOSOPHER/AUTHOR

Keep your temper. No one else wants it.

UNKNOWN

"Quaker Dozen"

1. Begin each day with a prayer
2. Work hard
3. Love your family
4. Make light of your troubles
5. Follow the Golden Rule
6. Read from the Bible
7. Show kindness
8. Read worthwhile books
9. Be clean and pure
10. Have charity in your heart
11. Be obedient and respectful
12. End the day in prayer

When you are at the end of your rope,
it's a good idea to keep your feet on the ground.

UNKNOWN

It's wonderful to be young...but remember that youth, with a
whole life before it, can make serious mistakes.

ECCLESIASTES 11:9-10 TLB

There are two things I've learned in life: You should never race a
guy named Rocky, and never bring a girl named Bubbles home to
meet your mother. Both of which I've done, by the way.

BURT REYNOLDS, ACTOR

SEEK GOOD ROLE MODELS

I had a very special contact with my parents which made life so alive! They encouraged me to try new things. They taught me that failure isn't wrong, that it was the lack of trying that was bad. By the time I was 16, I played lots of sports, six musical instruments, wrote for the school newspaper, sang in the school choral group. My father took me on business trips (his way of showing me the world from his shoulders). It was lovely, and I've never forgotten it. If I needed them, all I had to do was reach out.

DAVID HARTMAN

Children learn winning behavior best when their parents model it for them.

DR.HILLERY M. MOTSINGER

Paul, the apostle, said to young Timothy, "Don't let anyone look down on you because you are young, but set an example for the believers in speech, in life, in love, in faith and in purity."

I TIMOTHY 4:12

Children should seek a good role model like a honey bee seeks a beautiful flower.

ROBERT J. HALL

Follow my example, as I follow the example of Christ.

PAUL, THE APOSTLE, I CORINTHIANS 11:1

In Japan, where champions are expected to uphold the strictest codes of personal conduct, professional athletes are encouraged to make their hero-image a permanent way of life.

KAREN JUDSON, KIWANIS MAGAZINE

People seldom improve when they have no other model but themselves to copy after.

GOLDSMITH

You can model for your children wisely and well when you remember that they will be like the mountain climbers, following the guide up the mountain, who say, 'Please be careful. We are walking in your footsteps.' You model for your children best when you always, always remember: As you are, so will they be.

WAYNE DOSICK, GOLDEN RULES

The story goes that a fellow was walking past a cemetery when he noticed a tombstone with the following inscription:

As you are now, so once was I.
As I am now, you are sure to be.
So may I say, as now I lie,
Prepare yourself, to follow me.

The gentlemen took out a piece of chalk and wrote underneath the inscription:

To follow you I'm not content,
Until I know which way you went.

COACH JOHN WOODEN

WORK IS COMMANDED

The Lord God said to Adam, "By the sweat of your brow you will eat your food until you return to the ground, since from it you were taken; for dust you are and to dust you will return."

GENESIS 3: 19

The Apostle Paul instructed Christians:
For even when we were with you, we gave you this rule:
"If a man will not work, he shall not eat."

II THESSALONIANS 3:10

Work is a great blessing...after evil came into the world,
work was given as an antidote, not as a punishment.

ARTHUR S. HARDY

Hard work spotlights the character of people: some turn up their sleeves, some turn up their noses, and some don't turn up at all.

SAM EWING

Real success is finding your lifework in the work that you love.

DAVID MCCULLOUGH

If a man has any greatness in him, it comes to light—not in one flamboyant hour, but in the ledger of his daily work.

BERYL MARKHAM

Most footprints on the sands of time were left by work shoes.
UNKNOWN

Everything we do is merely practice work for something greater.
UNKNOWN

The biggest mistake you can make
is to believe you are working for someone else.
UNKNOWN

Never confuse activity with accomplishments.
Results is what counts.
COACH GENE STALLINGS

People who are busy helping others are never out of a job.
H. M. STANSIFER

When one finds himself in a hole of his own making,
it is a good time to examine the quality of workmanship.
JON REMMERDE

To do a job costs money. To redo it is a waste of money.
ALBERT LEOFFLER

Two monkeys were in a space capsule on their way to the moon.
One complained about the situation. The other said, "Well, it's
better than working in the cancer clinic."
DOC BLAKELY

Work as a Builder

Be a Builder

I watched them tearing a building down,
A gang of men in a busy town;
With a ho-heave-ho and a lusty yell
They swung a beam and a side wall fell.

I asked the foreman, "Are these men skilled,
As the men you'd hire if you had to build?"
He gave a laugh, and said, "No, indeed!
Just common labor is all I need."

"I can easily wreck in a day or two
What builders have taken years to do."
I thought to myself as I went my way,
Which of these roles have I tried to play?

Am I a builder who works with care,
Measuring life by the rule and square?
Am I shaping my deeds to a well-laid plan
Patiently doing the best I can?

Or am I a wrecker who walks the town
Content with the labor of tearing down?

Unknown

The lowly ant teaches us a great lesson about work—
Go to the ant, you sluggard; consider its ways and be wise!
It has no commander, no overseer or ruler, yet it stores its
provisions in summer and gathers its food at harvest.

PROVERBS 6:6-8

The work of the individual still remains
the spark that moves mankind forward.

IGOR SIKORSKY

Much effective work is done quietly, and with no outward sign.

UNKNOWN

As no true work since the world began was ever wasted,
so no true life since the world began has ever failed.

RALPH WALDO EMERSON

I Won't is a tramp. I Can't is a quitter. I Don't Know is lazy. I Wish
I Could is a wisher. I Might is waking up. I Will Try is on his feet.
I Can is on his way. I Will is at work. I Did is now the boss.

CALL WORKMAN

Foreman (on excavation job):
"Do you think you are fit for really hard labor?"

Applicant: "Well, some of the best judges
in the country have thought so."

UNKNOWN

PATIENCE SERVES YOU WELL

Patience is the guardian of faith, the preserver of peace, the cherisher of love, the teacher of humility. Patience governs the flesh, strengthens the spirit, sweetens the temper, stifles anger, extinguishes envy, subdues pride: she bridles the tongue, restrains the hand, tramples upon temptations, endures persecutions.

BISHOP HORNE

Face your deficiencies and acknowledge them; but do not let them master you. Let them teach you patience, sweetness, insight.

HELEN KELLER

Teach me Lord to wait right down on my knees till in your own good time to answer my pleas. Teach me not to rely on what others do, but to wait in prayer for an answer from you. Teach me, Lord. Teach me, Lord, to wait.

STUART HAMBLEN

But the fruit of the Spirit is love, joy, peace, patience, kindness, goodness, faithfulness, gentleness and self-control. Against such things there is no law.

GALATIANS 5:22-23

If you are patient in one moment of anger, you will escape 100 days of sorrow.

CHINESE PROVERB

"Have courage for the great sorrows of life and
patience for the small ones. And when you have finished
your daily task, go to sleep in peace. God is awake."

VICTOR HUGO

Patience serves as a protection against wrongs
as clothes do against cold. For if you put on more clothes,
as the cold increases it will have no power to hurt you. So in like
manner you must grow in patience when you meet with great
wrongs, and they will then be powerless to vex your mind.

LEONARDO daVINCI

Be patient like a setting hen. Good things are yet to be.

ROBERT J. HALL

Diamonds are nothing more than chunks of coal
that stuck to their jobs.

MALCOLM FORBES

A woman who has never seen her husband fishing
doesn't know what a patient man she married!

UNKNOWN

Patience is the ability to idle your motor
when you feel like stripping your gears.

BARBARA JOHNSON

Patience may be a virtue but it will never help a rooster lay an egg.

DR. LAURENCE J. PETER

GROW MENTALLY, SPIRITUALLY AND PHYSICALLY

The purpose of life is to be a growing, contributing human being.

UNKNOWN

Then he went down to Nazareth with them and was obedient to them. But his mother treasured all these things in her heart. And Jesus grew in wisdom and stature, and in favor with God and men.

LUKE 2: 51-52

It's important to keep trying to do what you think
is right no matter how hard it is or how often you fail.
You never stop trying. I'm still trying.

COACH JOHN WOODEN

The greatest waste of our natural resources is the number of people who never achieve their potential. Get out of that slow lane. Shift into that fast lane. If you think you can't, you won't. If you think you can, there's a good chance you will. Even making the effort will make you feel like a new person. Reputations are made by searching for things that can't be done and doing them.

UNITED TECHNOLOGIES CORP.

Big shots are little shots who kept on shooting.

CHRISTOPHER MORLEY

A college class was graduating on a hot and humid day. As the graduates walked across the platform and received their diplomas from the president, he smiled, shook their hands, and said loudly, "Congratulations!" Then, in a much lower voice, one that was firm and could be heard only by the graduates, he would say, "Keep moving." He was only trying to keep the line moving across the stage, but his words were good advice for a lifetime: "Keep moving." After every achievement—growing up, graduation, marriage, job promotion, even retirement—the best advice is, "Keep moving." Don't stop. Don't stagnate. There is more to life than you have found thus far. This is not the end; it is only the beginning. Keep moving.

UNKNOWN

Just as a baby learns to walk by trying time
and time again after each fall, so shall you grow mentally,
spiritually and physically. Keep trying.

ROBERT J. HALL

To grow tall spiritually, a man must first learn to kneel.

UNKNOWN

Psychiatrist: "Based on what you've told me about yourself, Mr. Jones, I'd say your problems stem from your compulsion to be an overachiever in everything you do. Jones: "Okay, doc. Just tell me what to do, and I'll work on it night and day.

UNKNOWN

YOUR CHOICES BECOME YOU

Choice, not chance, determines human destiny.

ELEANOR DOAN

The power of choice must involve the possibility of error—
that is the essence of choosing.

HERBERT SAMUEL

"...Then choose for yourselves this day whom you will serve, ...but
as for me and my household, we will serve the Lord."

JOSHUA 24:15

Choose always the way that seems the best, however rough it may
be; custom will soon render it easy and agreeable.

PYTHAGORAS

Between two evils, choose neither; between two goods, choose both.

TYRON EDWARDS

The measure of choosing well, is, whether a man likes
and finds good in what he has chosen.

CHARLES LAMB

When in doubt, ask yourself: WWJD?
(What would Jesus do?)

No one can serve two masters. Either he will hate the one
and love the other, or he will be devoted to the one and despise
the other. You cannot serve both God and Money.

MATTHEW 6:24

Important Choices You Must Make in Life:

Friends—They can build you up or lead you astray.

Dates—This is testing ground which ultimately
leads to courtship and marriage. Be careful.

Entertainment—Don't do anything you would be
ashamed to discuss with your parents.

Sex Outside Marriage—God forbids it. Remain a virgin until
you are married. Read Proverbs 7 and I Thessalonians 4:3-5.

Alcohol, Tobacco Products and Drugs—
Don't even think about it.

Education—A good education is vital to a happy,
productive life. Get it in a Christian environment.

Career—This is the third most important choice you must
make in life. Use your God-given talents and do what you enjoy.

Spouse—This is the second most important choice
you must make. Choose carefully and wisely.

Heaven or Hell—This is the most important choice in life.
Will you follow Christ or the devil?

ROBERT J. HALL

BE AN ENCOURAGER

Can we make it although faced with obstacles galore
YES...WE CAN!

Can we overcome defeats and be victorious once more
YES...WE CAN!

Can we change where needed, replacing good for bad
YES...WE CAN!

Can we find ideas and mentors to guide our path
YES...WE CAN!

Can we have the energy and stamina to persist as needed
YES...WE CAN!

Can we start where we are with what we have and still win big
YES...WE CAN!

Can we have fun and make some memories enroute
YES...WE CAN!

Can we decide today-start today-and be on our new, better way
YES...WE CAN!

MAMIE McCULLOUGH

People often worry that taking an ethical stand could hurt
their careers. It takes nerve, commitment—real guts—to tackle
so many of today's moral problems. Encourage the courageous,
so they'll have the will to carry on.

PRICE PRICHETT

Singer John Denver, giving a commencement speech to his old high school, said, "The best thing you have to offer the world is yourself. You don't have to copy anyone else. To achieve success is to be first, and that's being yourself." He recalled how, after high school, he went on to Texas Tech with the intention of becoming an architect. "But I quit to become a singer," he said. "Not one person said I was doing the right thing. But I knew, deep down inside, I was born to sing for people. Singing is the most joyful thing in the world for me. Listen to yourself. You'll always know what's right. That's how you find success as a human being. Don't be afraid to be who you are."

UNKNOWN

It was not until I became an adult that I really
learned one can do far more in life than one first thinks.
Reach for the stars, but keep your feet on the ground.

ROBERT J. HALL

The minister's wife was visiting a member of the
congregation, and mentioned, with particular pride, that her
daughter had won first prize in a music recital.

"I know just how you feel," said her hostess encouragingly.
"I remember how pleased we were when our pig
got the blue ribbon at the fair last year."

DOC BLAKLEY

Think encouraging thoughts, speak encouraging words,
and, most important of all, adopt an air of confident
expectancy toward those you are trying to help.

WHATSOEVER THINGS

OPPORTUNITIES DWELL IN PROBLEMS

The game of life is a lot like football.
You have to tackle your problems, block your fears,
and score your points when you get the opportunity.

LEWIS GRIZZARD, READERS DIGEST

Trials are not enemies of faith but are
opportunities to prove God's faithfulness.

UNKNOWN

We are all faced with a series of great opportunities
brilliantly disguised as impossible situations.

UNKNOWN

Be very careful, then, how you live—not as unwise but as wise,
making the most of every opportunity, because the days are evil.

EPHESIANS 5:15-16

An opportunist is a person who meets a wolf
in the woods and appears the next day in a fur coat.

UNKNOWN

Henry J. Kaiser of World War II ship-building fame had this to say,
"Problems are only opportunities in work clothes."

You will never face a problem that's not charged with opportunity.

UNKNOWN

Opportunity—Often it comes disguised
in the form of misfortune, or temporary defeat.

NAPOLEON HILL

Misfortune breeds opportunity—A dropped carton
of a dozen eggs provides a great opportunity for an
egg omelet supper with your next door neighbor.

ROBERT J. HALL

When one door closes, another opens, but we often
look so long and so regretfully upon the closed door that
we do not see the one that has opened for us.

ALEXANDER GRAHAM BELL

Opportunity may knock only once but
temptation keeps on pounding forever.

CAROLYN COATS

A little girl was late getting home from school. "I had to help
another girl," she explained. "What did you do?" asked the
mother. "Oh, I sat down and helped her cry."

UNKNOWN

As Woody Allen once said, "It is clear the future holds great
opportunities. It also holds pitfalls. The trick will be to avoid the
pitfalls, seize the opportunities, and get home by six o'clock.

You Create Opportunities

The golden opportunity you are seeking is in yourself.
It is not in your environment; it is not in luck or chance,
or the help of others; it is in yourself alone.

ORISON SWETT MARDEN

There is no security on this earth; there is only opportunity.

GEN. DOUGLAS MACARTHUR

A generation ago there were a thousand people to
every opportunity, while today there are a thousand
opportunities to every person.

HENRY FORD

Most successful men have not achieved their distinction
by having some new talent or opportunity presented to them.
They have developed the opportunity that was at hand.

BRUCE BARTON

Therefore, as we have opportunity, let us do good to all people,
especially to those who belong to the family of believers.

GALATIANS 6:10

A frequent saying used by my father, J. D. Hall, Jr., was,
"We didn't know it couldn't be done, so we just did it."

ROBERT J. HALL

Procrastination is opportunity's natural assassin.

VICTOR KIAM

One day I went to the hospital for my yearly shot
when I saw a guy in a bed. No one was visiting him.
So I went to give him some company. He seemed to have
a smile on his face when I was talking to him.

STEVE, 7TH GRADE

Small opportunities are often the beginning of great enterprises.

DEMOSTHENES

The man who finally gets the opportunity to have
the last word in an argument with his wife
usually ends with the words—"Yes, Dear."

ROBERT J. HALL

Colin Powell talked about America in his 1994 commencement
address at Howard University in these words: "You have been
given citizenship in a country like none other on earth, with
opportunities available to you like no where else on earth. What
will be asked of you is hard work. Nothing will be handed to you.
Use your education and your success in life to help those still
trapped in cycles of poverty and violence. Above all, never lose
faith in America. Its faults are yours to fix, not to curse."

Be Dependable!

Be as dependable as:

The sun rising in the east and setting in the west.

The swallows returning to Capistrano.

The need for a newborn baby to cry.

The geese migrating north in the springtime.

The itching of the avid deer hunter's trigger finger in the fall.

A mama bear protecting her cubs.

Jesus was in going to the cross.

ROBERT J. HALL

Maturity means dependability, keeping one's word
and coming through in a crisis. The immature are masters of the
alibi. They are confused and conflicted. Their lives are a maze of
broken promises, former friends, unfinished business and good
intentions that somehow never materialize.

ANN LANDERS

Your word is your bond—keep it!

UNKNOWN

Being dependable time after time builds a reputation of great worth.

ROBERT J. HALL

For the Lord loves the just and will not forsake his faithful (dependable) ones. They will be protected forever, but the offspring of the wicked will be cut off.

PSALMS 37:28

A dependable person indicates that he/she:

Takes responsibility for his/her own actions.

Recognizes the value of his/her commitment to others.

Considers long-term relationships more important
than personal convenience or gain.

Will correct a mistake as soon as possible without excuses.

Lives by the Golden Rule.

ROBERT J. HALL

My greatest ability is my dependability.

UNKNOWN

At Visador we had a company slogan: "Dependable, That's Us!"

ROBERT J. HALL

A six-year old was telling her friends how to behave at her birthday party, which her father planned to host and chaperon. "He's okay if you do what he tells you and when he hollers at you to sit down, you'd better not wait 'til you can find a chair."

DOC BLAKELY

MONEY IS A RESPONSIBILITY

Earning and managing money is a personal responsibility
just as birds scratch for their own food daily.

ROBERT J. HALL

In your early years of making money, live as frugally as possible
in order that you may invest as much as possible.

DR. R. C. SPROUL

People who want to get rich fall into temptation and
a trap and into many foolish and harmful desires that plunge them
into ruin and destruction. For the love of money is a root of all
kinds of evil. Some people, eager for money, have wandered from
the faith and pierced themselves with many griefs.

I TIMOTHY 6:9-10

Cars are a lousy investment. Keep your cars until they become
embarrassing to drive, unless they fall apart first.

MICHAEL MATTHEWS

No matter how hard you hug your money, it never hugs back.

MOM OF H. JACKSON BROWN, JR.

Remember that more marriages end as a result of
disagreements about money than any other reason.

UNKNOWN

A man's treatment of money is the most decisive test of his
character—how he makes it and how he spends it.

JAMES MOFFATT

Gaining independence: Many persons think that by hoarding
money they are gaining safety for themselves. If money is your
only hope for independence, you will never have it.
The only real security that a person can have in this world
is a reserve of knowledge, experience, and ability.
Without these qualities, money is practically useless.

HENRY FORD

Don't buy anything on your credit card
that you can't pay off in full the next month.

MICHAEL MATTHEWS

You can do a whole lot more with money than you can without it.

DEWEY GODFREY

What we give to the poor...is what we carry with us when we die.

PETER MARIN

"How is your daughter getting along in
her bookkeeping class at school?"

"Terrific. Now, instead of asking for her allowance,
she just bills us for it."

DOC BLAKELY

INVEST FOR THE FUTURE

The habit of saving is itself an education; it fosters every virtue,
teaches self-denial and cultivates a sense of order.

T. T. MUNGER

Start saving money now. People think in order to save a lot of
money, you have to make a lot of money. In reality, acquiring a
substantial sum of money requires only two things: time
and the discipline to consistently work toward a goal.

JACK HANSLIK

When investing money, seek advice from those who have expertise
in the area of your investment. Pay generously for that counsel.
Scrutinize carefully advice from those who are selling.

LEE EATON

People who make money extremely fast usually lose it
or spend it all. People who make money over a longer
period of time tend to keep it.

DAVID M. HARMON

Those who spend most of their time making and hoarding money
often find the things they want most cannot be bought.

MOM OF H. JACKSON BROWN, JR.

The accumulation of wealth is an insufficient reason for living.

DR. JAMES DOBSON,
WHAT WIVES WISH THEIR HUSBANDS KNEW ABOUT WOMEN

Never forget—Earthly treasures meet earthly needs;
heavenly treasures meet heavenly needs:

Do not store up for yourselves treasures on earth, where moth
and rust destroy, and where thieves break in and steal. But store
up for yourselves treasures in heaven, where moth and rust do not
destroy, and where thieves do not break in and steal.

MATTHEW 6:19-20

Try to teach your children about the magic of compounding.
You might be surprised at how interested children can become
in saving and investing when you show them how quickly money
can accumulate. The "Rule of 72" is useful for determining how
long it will take to double any investment. Simply divide the rate
of return from an investment into seventy-two, and you will have
the approximate period of time over which your investment will
double. But don't forget about taxes in your equation! Either
reduce the rate of return by the tax effect, or plan to pay the taxes
from some other source of cash.

MICHAEL MATTHEWS

There's a story about a man praying to God. He says,
"Lord, is it true that to you a minute is like a thousand years, and a
penny is like a thousand dollars?" The Lord says, "Yes."

Then the man asks, "Then can I have a penny?"
The Lord replies, "In a minute."

UNKNOWN

KEYS TO SUCCESS

Awareness is a major key to success. Keep your
radar finely tuned. You never know where a good idea will
come from or how far it will take you.

MOM OF H. JACKSON BROWN, JR.

Six essential qualities are the key to success:
sincerity, personal integrity, humility, courtesy, wisdom, charity.

DR. WILLIAM MENNINGER

Success seems to be largely a matter of
hanging on after others have let go.

WILLIAM FEATHER

By myself I can do nothing;
I judge only as I hear, and my judgment is just,
for I seek not to please myself but Him who sent me.

JOHN 5:30 NIV

More than ever, insight into tomorrow is the
difference between success and failure.

UNKNOWN

He has achieved success who has worked well,
laughed often and loved much.

ELBERT HUBBARD

There is a four-word formula for success that applies equally well to organizations or individuals: Make yourself more useful.

UNKNOWN

Success is a marathon, not a sprint.

UNKNOWN

Don't confuse fame with success. Madonna is one; Helen Keller is the other.

ERMA BOMBECK

I know the price of success—dedication, hard work and an unremitting devotion to the things you want to see happen.

FRANK LLOYD WRIGHT, AMERICAN ARCHITECT

The game is well worth the candle that may have to be burned far into the night. There is no feeling like the feeling of success.

J. PAUL GETTY

You know where you'd like to go, whether it's to a national championship in basketball or a particular goal in your business or life. You must also realize that this goal will be simply a by-product of all the hard work and good thinking you do along the way—your preparation. The preparation is where success is truly found.

COACH JOHN WOODEN

It's tough to climb the ladder of success, especially if you're trying to keep your nose to the grindstone, your shoulder to the wheel, your eye on the ball, and your ear to the ground.

UNKNOWN

SUCCESS IS UP TO YOU

If you wish to achieve worthwhile things in
your personal and career life, you must become
a worthwhile person in your own self-development.

BRIAN TRACY

The highest reward for a man's toil is not what he
gets for it, but what he becomes by it.

JOHN RUSKIN

True success cannot be achieved alone.
Share financial rewards with those who help you achieve it.

ROBERT J. HALL

Do not conform any longer to the pattern of this world,
but be transformed by the renewing of your mind.
Then you will be able to test and approve what God's will is—
His good, pleasing and perfect will.

ROMANS 12:2 NIV

An executive was asked what her formula for success was.
"It's very simple," she said. "Just ten simple two-letter words.
'If it is to be, it is up to me.'"

UNKNOWN

God doesn't ask that we be successful, only that we be faithful.

DONALD E. WILDMON

Success...seems to be connected with action. Successful men keep moving. They make mistakes, but they don't quit.

CONRAD HILTON

The men who try to do something and fail are infinitely better than those who try to do nothing and succeed.

LLOYD JAMES

The future belongs to those who are willing to make short-term sacrifices for long-term gains.

FRED A. MANSKE, SR.

Experience shows that success is due less to ability than to zeal. The winner is he who gives himself to his work, body and soul.

CHARLES BUXTON

A young father, proudly holding his infant son in his arms,
was lost in thought as his mind trailed off into
a daydream of happy anticipation of a successful future.
Suddenly he turned to his wife and said,
"You know, dear, I'm going to work hard,
and some day we are going to be rich."
His wife quickly replied, "We are already rich, dear.
We have each other. Some day maybe we'll have money."

BRAUDE'S HANDBOOK OF HUMOR

YOUR ATTITUDE IS YOUR CHOICE

It is your actions and attitude when you are
on your own that reflect what you really are.

MARTIN VANBEE

To keep an attitude from souring,
treat it like you would a cup of milk. Cool it off.

MAX LUCADO

The greatest discovery of my generation is that man can alter his
life style simply by altering his attitude of mind.

WILLIAM JAMES

Then choose for yourselves this day whom you will serve. . .But as
for me and my household, we will serve the Lord.

JOSHUA 24:15

A good attitude helps level the peaks and valleys of life.

ROBERT J. HALL

Abraham Lincoln was once taken to task by an associate
for his attitude toward his enemies: "Why do you try to make
friends of them? You should try to destroy them."

Lincoln replied gently, "Am I not destroying my enemies
when I make them my friends?"

Attitude

The longer I live, the more I realize the impact of attitude on life.
Attitude, to me, is more important than facts. It is more important
than the past, than education, than money, than circumstances,
than failures, than successes, than what other people think or say
or do. It is more important than appearance, giftedness or skill.
It will make or break a company...a church...a home. The remark-
able thing is we have a choice every day regarding the attitude we
will embrace for that day. We cannot change our past...we cannot
change the fact that people will act in a certain way. We cannot
change the inevitable. The only thing we can do is play on the one
string we have, and that is our attitude...I am convinced that
life is 10% what happens to me and 90% how I react to it.
And so it is with you...we are in charge of our Attitudes.

CHARLES SWINDOLL

We cannot direct the wind, but we can adjust our sails.

UNKNOWN

A positive attitude may not solve all your problems, but it will
annoy enough people to make it worth the effort.

HERM ALBRIGHT

Don't go around with a chip on your shoulder,
people might think it came off your head.

CHANGING TIMES

NEVER STOP LEARNING

The beautiful thing about learning is
nobody can take it away from you.

B. B. KING

Who so neglects learning in his youth
loses the past and is dead for the future.

EURIPIDES, Greek playwright, 5TH CENTURY B.C.

Let the wise listen and add to their learning,
and let the discerning get guidance.

PROVERBS 1:5

In a very real sense, people who have read good literature have
lived more than people who cannot or will not read...It is not true
that we have only one life to live; if we can read, we can live as
many more lives and as many kinds of lives as we wish.

S. I. HAYAKAWA

The most important outcome of education is to help students
become independent of formal education.

PAUL E. GRAY

Education is what a fellow gets reading the fine print
and experience is what he gets by not reading it.

UNKNOWN

No day in which you learn something is a complete loss.
DAVID EDDINGS

Live to learn and you will learn to live.
PORTUGUESE PROVERB

The school of hard-knocks often teaches us
things we refused to learn earlier in life.
ROBERT J. HALL

What is defeat? Nothing but education;
nothing but the first step to something better.
WENDELL PHILLIPS

There's always room for improvement.
It's the biggest room in the house.
MOM OF H. JACKSON BROWN, JR.

Anyone who stops learning is old, whether at twenty or eighty.
Anyone who keeps learning stays young.
The greatest thing in life is to keep your mind young.
HENRY FORD

All men who have turned out worth anything
have had the chief hand in their own education.
SIR WALTER SCOTT

"Son, I worry about you being at the bottom of the class."
"Don't worry, Dad, they teach you the same stuff at both ends."
UNKNOWN

SEEK KNOWLEDGE

The fear of the Lord is the beginning of knowledge,
but fools despise wisdom and discipline.

PROVERBS 1:7

For knowledge to become wisdom and for the soul to grow,
the soul must be rooted in God.

MOUNTFORD

Knowledge is like a garden: if it is not cultivated,
it cannot be harvested.

GUINEAN SAYING

Wisdom is the power to put our time
and our knowledge to the proper use.

THOMAS WATSON, FOUNDER OF IBM

The art and science of asking questions
is the source of all knowledge.

DR. ADOLF BERLE, AMERICAN SCHOLAR

Knowledge diligently sought and well used
is the fountainhead of a productive and rewarding life.

ROBERT J. HALL

Knowledge is the frontier of tomorrow.

DENIS WAITLEY, SEEDS OF GREATNESS

People don't care how much you know
until they know how much you care.
<small>UNKNOWN</small>

We owe almost all our knowledge not to those
who have agreed but to those who have differed.
<small>CHARLES CALEB COLTON</small>

A man of knowledge uses words with restraint,
and a man of understanding is even-tempered.
<small>PROVERBS 17:27</small>

Knowledge humbleth the great man,
astonishes the common man, puffeth up the little man.
<small>UNKNOWN</small>

Knowledge and timber should not be used until they are seasoned.
<small>OLIVER WENDELL HOLMES</small>

We are drowning in information, but starved for knowledge.
<small>JOHN NAISBITT, MEGATRENDS, 1984</small>

Nothing is as frustrating as arguing with someone
who knows what he's talking about.
<small>SAM EWING</small>

I'm in favor of lowering the voting age to fourteen. After all, that's
when they know everything.
<small>GARY APPLE</small>

THINK RIGHT TO BE RIGHT

Think positively. Think progressively. Think constructively.
Put wings on your thoughts! The measure of a person is in his
or her thoughts. "For as he thinks in his heart, so is he."
(Proverbs 23:7) This was Solomon's total of a man,
his strength or weakness, his courage or cowardice, his peace
or confusion and his happiness or gloom. He is what he thinks.

UNKNOWN

Just as the unit of human society is not a man or a woman,
but a man and a woman, so the basis of achievement is not
thought or action, but thought and action. Great positions are
filled, not by the thoughtless, but by those who think—and follow
up their thoughts by deeds. There are two main keys to success:
think and work. And the first is think.

B. C. FORBES

You can not always control circumstances,
but you can control your own thoughts.

CHARLES POPPLESTOWN

Whatever is true, whatever is honorable,
whatever is just, whatever is pure, whatever is lovely,
whatever is gracious...think about these things.

PHILLIPIANS 4:8

Without doubt the mightiest thought
the mind can entertain is the thought of God.

A. W. TOZER

Thinking makes us what we are. Negative thinking is
self-destructive. Positive thinking is self-creative. Think happiness
and we will be happy. Think misery and we will be miserable.

LEROY BROWNLOW

Discovery consists of seeing what everybody has seen
and thinking what nobody has thought.

ALBERT SZENT-GYÖRGYI

The greatest computer ever made
is located between your two ears. It's your brain; use it!

ROBERT J. HALL

The four-way test of the things we think, say or do:
Is it the truth? Is it fair to all concerned? Will it build good will
and better relationships? Will it be beneficial to all concerned?

ROTARY INTERNATIONAL MOTTO

A local college professor couldn't get a new mechanical gadget
assembled. He gave it to his yard man and within five minutes, it
was operating. "How did you do that so quickly when I couldn't
even figure where to start?" The yard man shrugged his shoulders
and said, "I can't read. Instructions were useless.
When you can't read, you have to think."

DOC BLAKELY

REAL THINKING IS HARD WORK

Thinking is the hardest work there is,
which is the probable reason why so few engage in it.

HENRY FORD

All the problems of the world could be settled easily if
men were only willing to think. The trouble is that men very
often resort to all sorts of devices in order not to think,
because thinking is such hard work.

THOMAS J. WATSON

Never be afraid to sit awhile and think.

LORRAINE HANSBERRY

When some people stop to think they merely stop.

B. M. STANSIFER

There are two ways to slice easily through life;
to believe everything or to doubt everything.
Both ways save us from thinking.

ALFRED KORZYBSKI, POLISH-AMERICAN LINGUIST (1879-1950)

Create in me a new clean heart, O God,
filled with clean thoughts and right desires.

PSALMS 51:10

Teach me how to think—not what.

MICHAEL MCKINLEY

It is nonsense to say there is not enough time to be fully informed...Time given to thought is the greatest time-saver of all.

NORMAN COUSINS

Brainstorming ideas with others helps to purify your thinking.

ROBERT J. HALL

I would rather have a mind opened by wonder
than one closed by belief.

GERRY SPENCE, HOW TO ARGUE AND WIN EVERY TIME

We all need time to be alone; to think, to dream, to wonder.

BILLIE ROARK

To achieve the marvelous,
it is precisely the unthinkable that must be thought.

TOM ROBBINS, JITTERBUG PERFUME

Stubbornness does have its helpful features.
You always know what you are going to be thinking tomorrow.

UNKNOWN

The boss encourages free thinking. In fact, he is for anything he
doesn't have to pay for.

GARY APPLE

PROGRESS ONLY COMES WITH CHANGE

The world hates change,
yet it is the only thing that has brought progress.

CHARLES FRANKLIN KETTERING

Change is what keeps us fresh and innovative. Change is what
keeps us from getting stale. Change is what keeps us young.

RICK PITINO

And he said: "I tell you the truth, unless you change and become
like little children, you will never enter the kingdom of heaven.

MATTHEW 18:3 NIV

There is nothing permanent except change.

HERACLITUS (540-475? B.C.)

Just because we cannot see clearly the end of the road,
that is no reason for not setting out on the essential journey. On
the contrary, great change dominates the world, and unless we
move with the change we will become its victims.

JOHN F. KENNEDY, THE NEW YORK TIMES, JULY 2, 1964

Childhood is a time of rapid change. Between the ages of
twelve and seventeen, a parent can age thirty years.

SAM LEVENSON, COMEDIAN

Change. Some people hate it. Many people fear it. Some people try to sleep through it. But a select few—the achievers in society—welcome the events that throw others into turmoil.

Unknown

There is nothing more difficult to take in hand, more perilous to conduct, or more uncertain in its success than to take the lead in the introduction of a new order of things.

Niccolo Machiavelli, "The Prince"

God, grant me the serenity to accept the things
I cannot change, the courage to change the things I can,
and the wisdom to know the difference.

Reinhold Niebuhr

It seems there was a pretzel stand out front of an office building in New York. One day, a man came out of the building, plunked down a quarter, and then went on his way, without taking a pretzel. This happened every day for three weeks. Finally, the old lady running the stand spoke up and said: "Sir, excuse me. May I have a word with you?" The fellow said: "I know what you're going to say. You're going to ask me why I give you a quarter every day and don't take a pretzel." And the woman said, "Not at all. I just want to tell you that the price is now 35 cents!"

The Executive Speechwriter

COURAGE OVERCOMES FEAR

Courage is the resistance to fear,
mastery of fear—not the absence of fear.

MARK TWAIN

Being scared to death—and saddling up anyway.

JOHN WAYNE

Doing what you are afraid to do.
There can be no courage unless you are afraid.

EDDIE RICKENBACKER

If I were asked to give what I consider the single most
useful bit of advice for all humanity, it would be this:
Expect trouble as an inevitable part of life and when it comes,
hold your head high, look it squarely in the eye and say,
"I will be bigger than you. You cannot defeat me."

ANN LANDERS

Any coward can praise Christ,
but it takes a courageous man to follow Him.

ELEANOR DOAN

It takes courage to do that which is right
even when others vilify you.

ROBERT J. HALL

Far better it is to dare mighty things, to win glorious triumphs,
even though checkered by failure, than to take rank with those
poor spirits who neither enjoy much nor suffer much, because
they live in the gray twilight that knows neither victory nor defeat.

THEODORE ROOSEVELT

My message to you...be courageous! I have lived a long time. I
have seen history repeat itself again and again. Always America
has come out stronger and more prosperous. Be as brave as your
parents before you. Have faith! Go forward!

THOMAS A. EDISON (LAST PUBLIC MESSAGE)

Courage is an outgrowth of who we are. Exterior supports may
temporarily sustain, but only inward character creates courage.

MAX LUCADO, THE APPLAUSE OF HEAVEN

Don't be impatient. Wait for the Lord, and he will come
and save you! Be brave, stouthearted and courageous.
Yes, wait and he will help you.

PSALM 27:14 TLB

LEADERSHIP REQUIRES VISION

Leadership is the capacity to translate vision into reality.

WARREN BENNIS

Leaders have two important characteristics: First, they are going somewhere; second, they are able to persuade other people to go with them.

DON BEVERIDGE

The very essence of leadership is, that you have to have a vision. It is a vision you articulate clearly and forcefully on every occasion. You can't blow an uncertain trumpet.

THEODORE HESBURGH PRESIDENT, NOTRE DAME UNIVERSITY

Thomas Winninger of the Winninger Resource Group believes that the two facets blended among all great leaders are: (1) their ability to perceive what could be done and what lies ahead, and (2) their ability to share this with others and encourage them to share in the same vision. Where there is no vision, the people perish.

PROVERBS

With a clear vision of the ultimate goal, a great leader will, in a timely manner, weave into a master plan the necessary and sufficient personnel and resources to achieve the desired goal.

ROBERT J. HALL

The sign on Ted Turner's desk: "Either lead,
follow or get out of the way!"

The task of the leader is to get his people from
where they are to where they have not been.

HENRY KISSINGER, FORMER U.S. SECRETARY OF STATE

A recent graduate from the U.S. Military Academy
at West Point was quite small. In fact, he had to wear thick
socks to meet the five foot, two inch height requirement. He was
a little guy, but a brilliant scholar. As second lieutenant, he drew
as his first command the roughest, toughest platoon in the entire
Army. When he assumed command, he mustered the platoon to
attention in front of him and said, "Men, there are two questions
we must settle immediately! Question number one, is there
anyone in this outfit who thinks he can whip me?"

The men stood rigidly at attention, giving no response,
so he put them at ease and repeated the question. Finally, the
regimental heavyweight champion, standing six-foot-seven and
weighing 274, stepped forward and said, "I believe I can whip you."

"Good," responded the young lieutenant. "You're my
First Sergeant. Now, question number two. Is there anyone
here who thinks he can whip my First Sergeant?"

EXECUTIVE SPEECHWRITER'S NEWSLETTER

REAL LEADERSHIP ENJOYS FOLLOWSHIP

Leadership requires followership and following
is an act of trust, faith in the course of the leader, and that faith
can be generated only if leaders act with integrity.

LAWRENCE MILLER

Ethics must begin at the top of an organization.
It is a leadership issue, and the chief executive must set the example.

EDWARD L. HENNESSEY, JR.

The great man shows his greatness by
the way he treats the little man.

MOM OF H. JACKSON BROWN

Leadership is the ability to get people to do
what they don't want to do and like it.

HARRY TRUMAN

Good leaders are like baseball umpires:
they go practically unnoticed when doing their jobs right.

BYRD BAGGETT, TAKING CHARGE

A successful leader motivates his people with a caring attitude
and a clear vision of the organization's objectives.

ROBERT J. HALL

A platoon leader doesn't get his platoon to go by getting up
and shouting and saying, "I am smarter. I am bigger. I am stronger.
I am the leader." He gets men to go along with him because
they want to do it for him and they believe in him.

DWIGHT DAVID EISENHOWER

The Lord is my shepherd, I shall not be in want. He makes me
lie down in green pastures, he leads me beside quiet waters, he
restores my soul. He guides me in paths of righteousness for his
name's sake. Even though I walk through the valley of the shadow
of death, I will fear no evil, for you are with me; your rod and staff,
they comfort me. You prepare a table before me in the presence
of my enemies. You anoint my head with oil; my cup overflows.
Surely goodness and love will follow me all the days of my life,
and I will dwell in the house of the Lord forever.

PSALMS 23 NIV

Sayings from the Bible are very often proved
out in business. For example, tell the boss what you
think of him—and the truth will set you free.

DOC BLAKELY

Wife (reading her husband's fortune on a weight card): "You are
dynamic, a leader of men, and admired by women for your good
looks and strength of character. It's got your weight wrong, too!"

JACOB M. BRAUDE

True Peace Comes From God

The enjoyment of good days is not an accident; it is an achievement. The pleasant life is always conditional and one of the
conditions is the pursuit of peace. "He who would love life
and see good days...let him seek peace and pursue it."

I Peter 3:10,11

Peace and pleasantness just go together in a cause
and effect relationship in which each promotes the other;
and the result is the enhancement of health.
So if we want health and happiness, seek peace and pursue it.

Leroy Brownlow

Blessed are the peacemakers, for they will be called sons of God.

Matthew 6:9 NIV

There is a place of quiet rest, near to the heart of God,

A place where sin cannot molest, near to the heart of God.

There is a place of comfort sweet, near to the heart of God,

A place where we our Savior meet, near to the heart of God.

There is a place of full release, near to the heart of God,

A place where all is joy and peace, near to the heart of God.

Cleland B. McAfee

How good are you at sowing seeds of peace?

MAX LUCADO

We have been the recipients of the choicest bounties
of heaven. We have been preserved, these many years, in peace
and prosperity. We have grown in numbers, wealth and power,
as no other nation has ever grown. But we have forgotten the
gracious hand which preserved us in peace, and multiplied and
enriched and strengthened us; and we have vainly imagined, in the
deceitfulness of our hearts, that all these blessings were produced
by some superior wisdom and virtue of our own. Intoxicated with
unbroken success, we have become too self-sufficient to feel the
necessity of redeeming and preserving grace, too proud to pray to
the God that made us! It behooves us, then, to humble ourselves
before the offended Power, to confess our national sins,
and to pray for clemency and forgiveness.

PRESIDENT ABRAHAM LINCOLN PROCLAMATION, APRIL 30, 1863

Peace is seeing a sunrise or a sunset and knowing whom to thank.

UNKNOWN

A perturbed mother said, "Preacher, what do you do
to get a teenager daughter out of hot water?"
"Try putting some dishes in it," was his peaceful answer.

LEROY BROWNLOW

Be Loyal

The seventh fruit of the Spirit is the word for standing fast,
for steadfastness. It is the quality of reliability, trustworthiness,
which makes a person one on whom we can utterly rely
and whose word will stand. Phillips translates this
fruit "fidelity." Barclay translates it as "loyalty."

JOHN M. DRESHCER

Thomas Jefferson said in hiring men that he considered these
three items: 1) Is he honest? 2) Will he work? 3) Is he loyal?

The virtue of loyalty may be compared to the cranes. They have a
king and they all serve him with more loyalty than is encountered
in any other animal. At night, when they go to sleep, they place
their king in the middle and they surround him and they always
send two or three among them to stand guard. And these, in order
not to fall asleep, keep a foot up in the air, while the other stands
on the ground. And in the foot which is up they always hold a
stone so that, should sleep surprise them, the stone would fall and
they would feel it. And this they do out of loyalty to one another to
protect their king and the other cranes who sleep.

THE JOY OF WORDS

Loyalty is the one thing a leader cannot do without.

A. P. GOUTHEY

Ethical leadership produces loyalty in followers.

ROBERT J. HALL

To Christ be loyal and be true; he needs brave
volunteers to stand against the powers of sin, moved not by
frowns or fears. To Christ be loyal and true; in noble service prove
your faith and your fidelity, the fervor of your love.

ELISHA A. HOFFMAN (1900)

Loyalty is more valuable than diamonds.

PHILIPPINE PROVERB

Remind the people to be subject (loyal)
to rulers and authorities, to be obedient,
to be ready to do whatever is good,
to slander no one, to be peaceable and considerate,
and to show true humility toward all men.

TITUS 3:1 NIV

Loyalty must arise spontaneously from the hearts of people
who love their country and respect their government.

JUSTICE HUGO L. BLACK

There are three ways whereby a man may become great: being
loyal, telling the truth and not thinking idle thoughts.

LONGINUS

Don't accept your dog's loyalty as
conclusive evidence that you are wonderful.

ANN LANDERS

Some Mistakes Annoy; Some Destroy

Mistakes That Annoy

These are mistakes of the head, not the heart.

ROBERT J. HALL

It's all right to make a mistake.
Just don't make the same mistake twice.

J. D. HALL, JR.

Future triumphs are often born from past mistakes.

UNKNOWN

A man should spend some time every day worrying about the
mistakes he has made—we recommend five seconds.

UNKNOWN

You can make mistakes, but you aren't a failure
until you start blaming others for those mistakes.
When you blame others you are trying to excuse yourself.

COACH JOHN WOODEN

The greatest mistake a man can make is to be afraid to make one.

ELBERT HUBBARD

Learn from the mistakes of others.
You may not live long enough to make them all yourself.

CAROLYN COATS

If you're headed in the wrong direction, God allows u-turns.

BUMPER STICKER

Mistakes That Destroy

The reputation of a thousand years
may be determined by the conduct of one hour.

JAPANESE PROVERB

Everybody makes honest mistakes,
but there's no such thing as an honest coverup.

PRICE PRITCHETT

A good, well-earned reputation can be destroyed
by just one mistake of passion.

ROBERT J. HALL

When tempted, no one should say, "God is tempting me." For God
cannot be tempted by evil, nor does he tempt anyone; but each
one is tempted when, by his own evil desire, he is dragged away
and enticed. Then, after desire has conceived, it gives birth to sin;
and sin, when it is full-grown, gives birth to death.

JAMES 1:13-15

Every married man should forget his mistakes.
No use two people remembering the same thing.

BRAUDE'S HANDBOOK OF HUMOR

GIVE GENEROUSLY

It is possible to give without loving,
but it is impossible to love without giving.

R. BRAUNSTEIN

Think It Over:

God made the sun—it gives.

God made the moon—it gives.

God made the stars—they give.

God made the air—it gives.

God made the clouds—they give.

God made the earth—it gives.

God made the sea—it gives.

God made the trees—they give.

God made the flowers—they give.

God made the fowls—they give.

God made the beasts—they give.

God made the Plan—He gives.

God made man—He . . . ?

SELECTED

If I can put one touch of rosy sunset into the life of any man or
woman, I shall feel that I have worked with God.

GEORGE MACDONALD

Nothing can give you greater joy
than doing something for another.
UNKNOWN

Remember this: Whoever sows sparingly will also reap sparingly,
and whoever sows generously will also reap generously. Each
man should give what he has decided in his heart to give, not
reluctantly or under compulsion, for God loves a cheerful giver.
II CORINTHIANS 9:6-7

In western Oklahoma an Indian Chief invited
his pale-faced guests to share in a huge pot of stew.
Generously he said, "Dig down deep, get puppy."
J. D. HALL, JR.

The best thing to give . . . to your enemy is forgiveness; to an
opponent, tolerance; to a friend, your heart; to your child, a good
example; to a father, deference; to your mother, conduct that will
make her proud of you; to yourself, respect; to all men, charity.
LORD BALFOUR

When we come to the end of life,
the question will be, "How much have you given?" not,
"How much have you gotten?" Do your givin' while you're livin'—
then you're knowin' where it's goin'.
UNKNOWN

YIELD NOT TO TEMPTATION

Temptation is sure to ring your doorbell,
but do not ask it to stay for dinner.

UNKNOWN

God is faithful; he will not let you be tempted beyond what you can
bear. But when you are tempted, he will also provide a way out...

I CORINTHIANS 10:13 NIV

You are not tempted because you are evil;
you are tempted because you are human.

UNKNOWN

Yield not to temptation, for yielding is sin; Each victory
will help you some other to win. Fight manfully onward, dark
passions subdue. Look ever to Jesus: He'll carry you through.

HORATIO R. PALMER (1868)

No man knows how bad he is until he has tried to be good. There is a
silly idea about that good people don't know what temptation means.

C. S. LEWIS THE SCREWTAPE LETTERS

Satan, like a fisher, baits his hook according to the appetite of the fish.

THOMAS ADAMS

Temptation provokes me to look upward to God.

JOHN BUNYAN

Temptations are like tramps. Treat them kindly
and they return bringing others with them.

THE LINK

Beware! Temptation is Satan's greatest weapon against you.

ROBERT J. HALL

Temptation is the tempter looking through the keyhole into the
room where you are living; sin is your drawing back the bolt
and making it possible for him to enter.

J. WILBUR CHAPMAN

Some temptations come to the industrious,
but all temptations attack the idle.

CHARLES HADDON SPURGEON

Following the path of least resistance
makes both rivers and men crooked.

UNKNOWN

There was never any one so good that he was exempt
from trials and temptations.

ANONYMOUS

Middle age is when you're faced with two temptations and you
choose the one that will get you home by 9 o'clock.

RONALD REAGAN

Be Humble Like Jesus

Truly great people are always humble—like Jesus.

UNKNOWN

And being found in appearance as a man,
he (Jesus) humbled himself and became obedient.

PHILIPPIANS 2:8 NIV

Blessed is the servant who accepts rebuke with courtesy, obeys
respectfully, confesses humbly, and makes amends gladly.

UNKNOWN

I believe the first test of a truly great man is his humility.

JOHN RUSKIN

The humblest citizen of all the land, when clad in the armor of a
righteous cause, is stronger than all the hosts of error.

WILLIAM JENNINGS BRYAN

Six essential qualities are the key to success: sincerity,
personal integrity, humility, courtesy, wisdom, charity.

DR. WILLIAM MENNINGER

Humility like darkness reveals the heavenly lights.

HENRY D. THOREAU

And Jesus said, "I tell you the truth, unless you change and
become like children, you will never enter the kingdom of heaven.
Therefore, whoever humbles himself like this child
is the greatest in the kingdom of heaven.

MATTHEW 18: 3-4 NIV

Toot your own horn and the notes will be flat.

MAX LUCADO

Humility is such a frail and delicate thing that he who dares to think
that he has it, proves by that single thought that he has it not.

IVAN O. MILLER

Someone has said in jest, "It is hard to be humble when
you are as great as I am," but let it be known that humility and
boasting are opposites just like north and south.

ROBERT J. HALL

What does the Lord require of you? To act justly,
to love mercy and to walk humbly with your God.

MICAH 6:8 NIV

Mothers and fathers who think they're important
should remind themselves that this country honors each of them
only one day of the year. Pickles get a whole week.

UNKNOWN

BE GUIDED BY MORAL STANDARDS

The Christian religion is the only one that puts morality
on its proper and right basis: the fear and love of God.

SAMUEL JOHNSON

The truly educated person recognizes some great moral truths.
These truths are like the North Star in determining our general
direction of daily life: Kindness is better than cruelty, honesty
is better than lying, education is better than ignorance, courage
better than cowardice. How these moral truths play themselves out
among competing interests and values make life exciting,
difficult and dangerous. But great moral truths of this
nature no truly educated person can ignore.

ROBERT PRIMACK, EDUCATOR

When evangelist Billy Graham was asked to give the invocation at
President Bush's inauguration, he cited this quotation by George
Washington: "America stands on two great pillars—faith and
morality. Without these, our foundation crumbles."

The people of our nation and the people of the whole world need
to be gripped by the moral imperatives which grow out of the
nature of God, by a sense of right, by principles of truth, and by
ideals of decency. Nothing is more needed by this sinful world
than a revival of simple goodness and genuine uprightness.

CLIFTON J. ALLEN POINTS FOR EMPHASIS

High moral standards help a person
avoid foolish, embarrassing deeds.

ROBERT J. HALL

Do not be fooled: You cannot cheat God. A person
harvests only what he plants. If he plants to satisfy his sinful self,
his sinful self will bring him eternal death. But if he plants to
please the Spirit, he will receive eternal life from the Spirit.

GALATIANS 6:7-8 ICB

All moral obligation resolves itself into
the obligation of conformity to the will of God.

CHARLES HODGE

To give a man full knowledge of true morality,
I would send him to no other book than the New Testament.

JOHN LOCKE

One of the candidates for sheriff in a small
South Carolina town was notorious for his dishonesty. When my
seamstress told me she was going to vote for him, I asked why,
since his opponent was a man of unquestionable morals.

"Well," she said, "I looks at it this way—if a man ain't
ruint when he goes into office, he's ruint when he comes out.
And there ain't no use in ruinin' a good man."

MRS. B. W. LANEY

HUMOR BRIGHTENS YOUR DAY

Good humor is an avenue to self-esteem, and the ultimate
type of humor is the rich ability to laugh at yourself.

SENATOR ALAN K. SIMPSON

"Here," said Johnny to his father, "is my report card." "And here," he
added triumphantly, "is an old one of yours I found in the attic."

UNKNOWN

You cannot hold back a good laugh any more than
you can the tide. Both are forces of nature.

WILLIAM ROTSLER

I'm seeing that a sense of humor is perhaps the
only way God has put up with us for so long.

MAX LUCADO

Laughter is the lotion for the sunburns in your life.

DOC WHITE

The reason the cow jumped over the moon was because
there was a short circuit in the milking machine.

UNKNOWN

Remember—The best person to laugh at is yourself.

ROBERT J. HALL,

There is a time for everything, and a season for every activity
under heaven: a time to weep and a time to laugh.

ECCLESIASTES 3:1,4

When I was a student, I fell in love with my history teacher. So one
day I asked for a date. She said, "Fine. How about 1776."

UNKNOWN

Hearty laughter is a good way to
jog internally without having to go outdoors.

NORMAN COUSINS

Birds of a feather flock to a newly washed car.

UNKNOWN

Two men were climbing a particularly difficult mountain when
one of them suddenly fell down a crevasse 500 feet deep. "Are
you all right, Bert?" called the man at the top of the crevasse.
"I'm still alive, thank goodness, Fred," came the reply. "Here, grab
this rope," said Fred, throwing a rope down to Bert. "I can't grab
it," shouted Bert. "My arms are broken." "Put the rope in your
mouth," shouted Fred. So Bert put the rope in his mouth and Fred
began to haul him to safety. 490 feet...400 feet...300 feet...200
feet...100 feet...50 feet...and then Fred called out, "Hey, Bert, how
are you doing?" Bert replied, "I'm fi...ahhhhhh!"

THE EXECUTIVE SPEECHWRITER NEWSLETTER

STRETCH FOR YOUR DREAMS

Nothing happens unless first a dream

CARL SANDBURG

It isn't a bad thing to be a dreamer,
provided you are awake when you dream.

UNKNOWN

Keep true to the dreams of your youth.

JOHANN SCHILLER

All men who have achieved great things have been dreamers.

ORISON SWETT MARDEN

And it shall come to pass afterward, that I will pour out my spirit
upon all flesh; and your sons and your daughters shall prophesy,
your old men shall dream dreams, your young men shall see visions.

JOEL 2:28

Some men see things as they are and say "Why?"
I dream things that never were, and say, "Why not?"

GEORGE BERNARD SHAW

One day Michelangelo saw a block of marble which the owner said
was of no value. "It is valuable to me," said Michelangelo.
"There is an angel imprisoned in it and I must set it free."

UNKNOWN

Success is a dream turned into reality.

UNKNOWN

Like small creeks that grow into mighty rivers,
the dreams of leaders eventually shape the course of history.

UNKNOWN

When you dream reach for the stars,
but don't be surprised if you land on the moon.

ROBERT J. HALL

The future belongs to those who believe in the beauty of their dreams.

ELEANOR ROOSEVELT

A number two pencil and a dream can take you anywhere.

UNKNOWN

Outstanding leaders are future-oriented. They love to dream
about what could be and to involve others in their dreams.

UNKNOWN

Always dream and shoot higher than you know you can reach.
Don't bother just to be better than your contemporaries and
predecessors—try to be better than yourself.

UNKNOWN

"My wife had a dream last night and thought she was married to
a millionaire." "You're lucky! My wife thinks that in the daytime."

HERBERT V. PROCHNOW

VISION + WORK CLOTHES = SUCCESS

A vision without a task is a dream; A task without a vision is drudgery; A vision and a task is the hope of the world.

ANONYMOUS

Dreams may be broad and bold. Vision must be focused and specific. Success demands hard work and determination.

ROBERT J. HALL

Where there is no vision, the people perish.

PROVERBS 29:18

Vision is of God. A vision comes in advance of any task well done.

KATHERINE LOGAN

The empires of the future are empires of the mind.

WINSTON CHURCHILL

The most pathetic person in the world is someone who has sight but has no vision.

HELEN KELLER (1880-1968), AMERICAN ESSAYIST

Give us clear vision that we may know where to stand and what to stand for, because unless we stand for something, we shall fall for anything.

PETER MARSHALLMR. JONES, MEET THE MASTER

Poor eyes limit your sight; poor vision limits your deeds.

FRANKLIN FIELD

Every day after school Giovanni would rush to Michelangelo's studio to watch the famous sculptor chip away at a 14-foot high block of marble. Week after week, the boy came and watched, as the magnificent form of David began to take shape. Finally, it was done. The boy was absolutely amazed by the transformation of a piece of stone into the beautiful David, and, in all innocence, he said to Michelangelo, "How did you know he was in there?"

Michelangelo knew because he had a vision of what he could create, if he was willing to dedicate himself to it— if he was willing to take risks—if he was willing to work hard enough and long enough until his vision was a reality.

EXECUTIVE SPEECHWRITER

Cherish your visions and your dreams as they are the children of your soul; the blue prints of your ultimate achievements.

NAPOLEON HILL

Ah, but a man's reach should exceed his grasp, or what's a heaven for?

ROBERT BROWNING, poet

I tell my children not to despair if all their dreams come out wrong. It might mean they have a future in weather forecasting.

DOC BLAKELY

Prayer is Quiet Time With God

Prayer is releasing the energies of God.
For prayer is asking God to do what we cannot do.

CHARLES TRUMBULL

A meaningful prayer life is essential in maintaining a Christ-centered home. Being able to bow in prayer as the day begins or ends gives expression to the frustrations and concerns that might not otherwise be ventilated. On the other end of the prayer line is a loving heavenly Father who has promised to hear and answer our petitions.

DR. JAMES DOBSON, LOVE FOR A LIFETIME

Do not be anxious about anything, but in everything, by prayer and petition, with thanksgiving, present your requests to God.

PHILIPPIANS 4:6 NIV

Prayer is the tiny nerve that moves God's mighty hand.

UNKNOWN

Essentially, prayer is based on a relationship. We don't converse freely with someone we don't know. We bare our souls and disclose our hidden secrets only to someone we trust.

UNKNOWN

Prayer is the unfolding of one's will to God that He may fulfill it.

SAINT THOMAS AQUINAS

There is only one limit to what prayer can do;
that is what God can do.

R. A. TORREY

As Jesus prayed for guidance and strength, we,
too, must submit our will to the Lord in prayer.

ROBERT J. HALL

Satan trembles when he sees the weakest Christian on his knees.

UNKNOWN

Our prayer and God's mercy are like two buckets in a well;
while one ascends the other descends.

HOPKINS

Prayer is a ladder on which thoughts mount to God.

ABRAHAM J. HESCHEL

If prayer does not drive sin out of your life,
sin will drive prayer out.

UNKNOWN

It is impossible to overstate the need
for prayer in the fabric of family life.

DR. JAMES DOBSON, LOVE FOR A LIFETIME

From up in his bedroom, a 6-year-old yelled,
"I'm gonna say my prayers now. Does anyone want anything?"

UNKNOWN

WHEN WE PRAY GOD HEARS US

But when you pray, go into your room, close
the door and pray to your Father, who is unseen. Then your
Father, who sees what is done in secret, will reward you.

MATTHEW 6:6

The best way for a child to learn to pray is to live with a father and
mother who know a life of friendship with God, and who truly pray.

JOHANN HEINRICH PESTALOZZI

A child once prayed, "O, Lord, make the bad people good,
and the good people nice."

UNKNOWN

The greater your cares, the more genuine your prayers.

MAX LUCADO

All heaven listens when we send up
a heartfelt prayer for an enemy's good.

BLASTS FROM THE RAM'S HORN

If you are too busy to pray, you are busier than you ought to be.

UNKNOWN

Heed the advice of Francis Cardinal Spellman:
"Pray as if everything depended on God
and work as if everything depended on man."

When the searchers found a five-year-old boy
who had been lost in the mountains for two days, they asked,
"Were you afraid?" "It was scary," the little boy answered,
"but I prayed and God took good care of me.

UNKNOWN

Here's the prayer of a child: "And, dear God,
I hope You'll also take care of Yourself. If anything
should happen to You, we'd be in an awful fix."

UNKNOWN

If stress and strife of the times causes us to become
weak-kneed, perhaps we should let them collapse entirely and
while in that position do a little serious praying.

UNKNOWN

Do not pray for easy lives; pray to be stronger people! Do not pray
for tasks equal to your powers; pray for power equal to your tasks.

PHILLIPS BROOKS

A grandfather was going by his little granddaughter's room one
night when he saw her kneeling beside her bed, head bowed and
hands folded, repeating the alphabet. "What are you doing?" he
asked her. She explained, "I'm saying my prayers, but I couldn't
think of just what I wanted to say. So I'm saying all the letters, and
God can put them together however he thinks best."

UNKNOWN

BE A PROBLEM SOLVER

Every person has a unique problem, and it is a rather
tough problem, too. That problem is life. What are you going to do
about it? If you do not know what you are going to do with life, life
will do something to you—that is a fact. Either you will master
life or life will master you. It is just that simple.

Whatever problems you may be facing, you can solve
them, if you will trust yourself and believe in your capacity to
do it. If you haven't the know-how, you can get it. If you lack the
insight, you can find it. If you do not have the wisdom, you can
obtain it. And as long as you are alive, you can do something
about the everyday problems that come with life.

UNKNOWN

The only difference between a problem and a solution is that
people understand the solution.

CHARLES KETTERING

All of us might as well swap problems because
we all know exactly how to solve other people's problems.

UNKNOWN

Solving problems is most often a step by
step process reaching toward clearly defined goals.

ROBERT J. HALL

And when they could not come near Him because of the crowd,
they uncovered the roof where He was. So when they had broken
through, they let down the bed on which the paralytic was lying.

MARK 2:4

Problems are things that you solve, not reasons to avoid action.

UNKNOWN

The challenges are huge, but we should face them with the same
confidence that David displayed when he faced the giant Goliath.
Everyone advised David to forget about confronting the enormous
giant, saying, "He's so huge, there's no way you can win." To which
David replied, "He's so huge, there's no way I can miss."

UNKNOWN

Each problem has hidden in it an opportunity
so powerful that it literally dwarfs the problem. The greatest
success stories were created by people who recognized a
problem and turned it into an opportunity.

JOSEPH SUGARMAN

Three men were arguing over which profession was the oldest.
Said the surgeon: "The Bible says Eve was made by carving a rib
out of Adam. I guess that makes mine the oldest profession."

"Not at all," said the engineer. "In six days the earth
was created out of chaos—and that was an engineer's job."

Said the politician: "Yes, but who created chaos?"

DOC BLAKELY

BE OPTIMISTIC AND ENJOY LIFE

An optimistic person is one who cheerfully expects
things to work out all right in the future.

S. I. HAYAKAWA

Optimism is the sunshine in our souls.

ROBERT J. HALL

A healthy realism about your own abilities should be
matched by an irrepressible optimism about God's.

WORD PUBLISHING

Not that we are sufficient of ourselves to think of anything as
being from ourselves, but our sufficiency is from God.

2 CORINTHIANS 3:5

May I never miss a rainbow or a sunset because I am looking down.

UNKNOWN

A successful man is one who has the horsepower of
an optimist and the emergency brakes of a pessimist.

UNKNOWN

Many an optimist has bought out a pessimist and became rich.

B. M. STANSIFER

Keep your face to the sunshine
and you cannot see a shadow.

HELEN KELLER

A historian has pointed out that the secret of our national
greatness is the fact that optimists from all over the world came to
America. The people who came here were those who believed in
the future. They had the daring to break old ties and launch forth
into the unknown. They left the pessimists standing on the dock in
the homeland afraid to come along on the great adventure.

It is well to remember the mighty heritage of optimism that
is ours when defeatists begin to predict disaster. This nation was
built by optimists who believed in freedom and put their trust in
God. They have thrown us the torch of dynamic optimism—
it is up to us to keep it burning.

WILFERD PETERSON

Optimistic and unshaken thinking has the power to open new
worlds to us: a world of opportunity, a world of usefulness, a world
of health, a world of happiness and many others. The entrance to
them has always been through the avenue of positive thinking.

LEROY BROWNLOW

Optimist—one who thinks he will never do anything stupid again.

UNKNOWN

BE TRUSTWORTHY

If you want to be given trust, prove yourself trustworthy.
WORD PUBLISHING

How does one become trustworthy? It is earned! ALWAYS be
dependable and reliable in everything you say or do.
ROBERT J. HALL

The passengers on the train were uneasy as they sped along
through the dark, stormy night. The lightening was flashing,
black clouds were rolling and the train was traveling fast.
The fear and tension among the passengers was evident.

One little fellow, however, sitting all by himself, seemed
utterly unaware of the storm or the speed of the train.
He was amusing himself with a few toys.

One of the passengers spoke to him. "Sonny, I see you are alone on
the train. Aren't you afraid to travel alone on such a stormy night?"

The lad looked up with a smile and answered,
"No, ma'am, I ain't afraid. My daddy's the engineer."
BRETHREN QUARTERLY

With the public trust, everything is possible;
without it, nothing is possible.
ABRAHAM LINCOLN

Trust, like the soul, never returns, once it is gone.

<small>PUBLILIUS SYRUS: SENTENTIAE</small>

A gossip betrays a confidence, but a trustworthy man keeps a secret.

<small>PROVERBS 11:13</small>

A leader, particularly a teacher or coach, has a most
powerful influence on those he or she leads, perhaps
more than anyone outside of the family.

I consider it a sacred trust: helping to mold character,
instill productive principles and values, and provide a positive
example to those under my supervision.

Furthermore, it is a privilege to have that responsibility,
opportunity, and obligation, one that should never be taken lightly.

<small>COACH JOHN WOODEN</small>

"I am going away for a few days, Bridget," said the lady
of the house to her servant girl, "and I am going to leave with
you all my keys, those to my closets as well as those to my chests
and jewel boxes. I know that they will be safe with you, but,
of course, I expect you not to touch them."

When the mistress returned, the girl said to her,
"Madam, I'm going to leave you."

"Why, Bridget?"

"Because you don't trust me."

"How can you say that, when I left you with all my keys?"

"That you did, ma'am; but not one of them fits."

<small>BRAUDE'S HANDBOOK OF HUMOR</small>

LET THE BIBLE BE YOUR GUIDE

This great book (the Bible) is the best gift God has given
to man, but for it we could not know right from wrong.

ABRAHAM LINCOLN

All Scripture is given by inspiration of God, and
is profitable for doctrine, for reproof, for correction, for
instruction in righteousness, that the man of God may be
complete, thoroughly equipped for every good work.

2 TIMOTHY 3:16, 17 NKJV

The Bible is a book of faith, and a book of doctrine, and a book
of morals, and a book of religion, of special revelation from God;
but it is also a book which teaches man his own individual responsibility, his own dignity, and his equality with his fellow man.

DANIEL WEBSTER, JUNE 17, 1843

So great is my veneration for the Bible that the earlier
my children begin to read it, the more confident will be my
hope that they will prove useful citizens to their country,
and respectable members of society.

JOHN QUINCY ADAMS

As Billy Graham once said, "I've read the
last page of the Bible. It's going to turn out all right."

As the young calf eagerly searches for his mother's milk, so too, must children turn to the Bible for guidance in a troubled world.

ROBERT J. HALL

Everything from handling money to sexual attitudes is discussed in Scripture, with each prescription bearing the personal endorsement of the King of the Universe. Why would anyone disregard this ultimate resource?

DR. JAMES DOBSON, LOVE FOR A LIFETIME

God's Word, the Bible, is the world's only completely trustworthy measuring stick for truth. Without the Bible there is no absolute standard for right or wrong.

BOBB BIEHL, WISDOM FOR MEN

In one of his house calls, the preacher asked for the family Bible, wanting to read a passage. Then they called in the children and organized a hunt for the Good Book. At last one of the children dug up a few wrinkled pages of Holy Scripture. The father took the pages and triumphantly handed them to the preacher.

"This is no Bible," protested the preacher.

The man argued, "Yes, it is, but I didn't know we were so nearly out."

LEROY BROWNLOW

The Word of God is our chart and compass. Without it, we lose our way.

HOPE POINTS THE WAY

Hope is the last thing that dies in man. While we
are traveling through life it conducts us in an easier
and more pleasant way to our journey's end.

FRANCOIS DE LA ROCHEFOUCAULD

Everything that was written in the past was written
to teach us, so that we could have hope. That hope comes from the
patience and encouragement that the Scriptures give us.

ROMANS 15:4 ICB

The resurrection of Jesus Christ is our hope today. It is our
assurance that we have a living Saviour to help us live as we should
now, and that when, in the end, we set forth on that last great
journey, we shall not travel an uncharted course, but rather we
shall go on a planned voyage—life to death to eternal living.

RAYMOND MACDENDREE QUEENS' GARDENS

Life with Christ is an endless hope, without Him a hopeless end.

ANONYMOUS

Make no little plans. They have no magic to stir men's blood.
Make big plans: aim high in hope and work.

DANIEL HUDSON BURNHAM

Everything that is done in the world is done by hope. No farmer
would sow one grain of corn if he hoped not it would grow up
and become seed; no bachelor would marry a wife if he hoped not
to have children; no merchant or tradesman would set himself to
work if he did not hope to reap benefit thereby.

MARTIN LUTHER: TABLE TALK

I have often been asked when I first started dreaming
about winning a national championship.

What I was dreaming about each year was trying to produce
the best basketball team we could be. My thoughts were directed
toward preparation, our journey (not winning national champi-
onships). That would simply have shifted my attention to the
wrong area, hoping for something out of my control.
Hoping doesn't make it happen.

COACH JOHN WOODEN

Hope is like a shadow; it is real but by itself it can do nothing.

ROBERT J. HALL

It was Mrs. Shiplett's first ocean voyage, and she was
deathly ill. Wanting to comfort her as much as he could, the
steward told her: "Don't be so downhearted, lady, I have
never heard of anyone dying of seasickness."

"Oh, don't tell me that," was her reply,
"it's only hope of dying that has kept me alive so far."

BRAUDE'S HANDBOOK OF HUMOR

HUMOR KEEPS YOU GOING

Humor is the great thing, the saving thing. The minute
it crops up, all our irritations and resentments slip away,
and a sunny spirit takes their place.

MARK TWAIN

I could not tread these perilous paths in safety,
if I did not keep a saving sense of humor.

LORD NELSON

Humor is everywhere you look. A sign was above a clock
in a cafe just off the square in Columbia, Tennessee:

This clock will never be stolen. Too many employees are watching it.

MOM OF H. JACKSON BROWN

The wicked plot against the righteous and gnash their teeth at
them; but the Lord laughs at the wicked, for he knows their day is
coming.

PSALMS 37:12-13

If you lose the power to laugh, you lose the power to think.

CLARENCE DARROW

A laugh is a smile that bursts!

UNKNOWN

"Allow me to congratulate you. I'm sure you will always look upon this as the happiest day of your life."

"But I'm not getting married until tomorrow."

"Yes, I know."

YOURS TRULY

Humor, you can't exist without it. You have to be able to laugh at yourself. Otherwise, you suffer.

KIRK DOUGLAS

My attitude toward my chosen profession is:
If I have caused just one person to wipe a tear of laughter, that's my reward. The rest goes to the government.

VICTOR BORGE

You must keep a sense of humor and be able to laugh at yourself. Have you heard the story of Oral Roberts, Billy Graham, and Robert Schuller? The story goes that they all died earlier than planned. Peter met them at the gate: "I'm sorry, guys. Your rooms aren't ready yet. You'll have to wait downstairs in hell until your room is ready." Before long, Satan called and said, "Peter, hurry up and get these guys out of here. Oral Roberts is healing the sick. Billy Graham's saving all the souls, and Robert Schuller's raising money to air-condition the place!"

ROBERT SCHULLER

Ad: "Weight Watchers will meet Tuesday at 7 PM at the Presbyterian Church. Please use the double door at the side entrance."

TRUTH COMES FROM GOD

God is truth, and light His shadow.

PLATO

What we have in us of the image of God is the love of truth and justice.

DEMOSTHENES

Truth is what God says about a thing.

SPEAKER'S SOURCEBOOK

Ye shall know the truth, and the truth shall make you free.

JOHN 8:32

Who speaks the truth stabs falsehood to the heart.

JAMES RUSSELL LOWELL

Of all duties, the love of truth, with faith and constancy in it, ranks first and highest. To love God and to love truth are one and the same.

SILVIO PELLICO

To love truth for truth's sake is the principal part of human perfection in this world, and the seed-pot of all other virtues.

LOCKE

A lie has speed, but truth has endurance.

EDGAR J. MOHN

In its purest form, truth is not a polite tap on the shoulder.
Truth is a howling reproach. What Moses brought down
from Mount Sinai were not ten suggestions.

TED KOPPEL, MODERATOR OF NIGHTLINE

The path of truth is the path of progress.

HAROLD LE CLAIRE ICKES

Truth is stronger than power and might.

ROBERT J. HALL

It is twice as hard to crush a half-truth as a whole lie.

AUSTIN O'MALLEY

If it is the truth what does it matter who says it.

ANONYMOUS

Truth is not only violated by falsehood;
it may be equally outraged by silence.

HENRI FRÉDÉRIC AMEIL

Truth does not consist in minute accuracy of detail,
but in conveying a right impression; and there are vague ways
of speaking that are truer than strict facts would be. When the
Psalmist said, "Rivers of water run down mine eyes,
because men keep not thy law," he did not state the fact,
but he stated a truth deeper than fact, and truer.

HENRY ALFORD

YOU MUST BE TRUTHFUL

Early on I discovered my father would not tolerate lying. When I "fessed up" and told the truth about my wrongdoings, I found him strangely charitable; but whenever I lied I discovered this same man could be most uncharitable. Dad hated lying. He was not going to have it (especially from his son). Later on I would learn that my dad and God shared a common view in regard to telling the truth.

JOHN GIPSON

The Lord detests lying lips,
but he delights in men who are truthful.

PROVERBS 12: 22

Tell the truth. That way you don't have to remember a story.

COACH JOHN WOODEN

Always, always, always be true to yourself.

UNKNOWN

Peace if possible, but truth at any rate.

MARTIN LUTHER

The greatest homage we can pay to truth is to use it.

RALPH WALDO EMERSON

We cannot forever hide the truth about ourselves, from ourselves.

JOHN McCAIN

Truth exists; only falsehood has to be invented.

JACQUES BRAQUE, ARTIST

Truth can hurt so wrap it in a blanket of love.

ROBERT J. HALL

Tell the truth because it is the smartest thing to do, and people will begin to believe you. Keep telling the truth, all of it, and people will believe you. Some will say that you can't tell the whole truth. That's hogwash. If two people know something, it's public, and all of it will be told sooner or later. Tell it all, and you surprise and make believers out of people. Honesty is so rare it's perhaps the most effective weapon available. Tell it all, and tell it first, and you get the best shot at the world. Hold it back, any of it, and you'll be trying to play 'catch up,' and you'll never really make it.

FRANK WYLIE,
DIRECTOR OF PUBLIC RELATIONS, CHRYSLER CORPORATION

It is strange but true; for truth is always strange, stranger than fiction.

GEORGE GORDON BYRON (LORD BYRON)

A patient came into the doctor's office for an examination the other day and, after it was over, the fellow said: "All right, Doc. Now I don't want you to give me a bunch of tongue twisting scientific talk. Just tell me truthfully in plain English what my problem is."

"All right," said the physician, "you're fat and you're lazy."

"Fine," said the patient, "now give me the scientific terms so I can tell my friends."

DOC BLAKELY

PAUSE TO REFRESH YOURSELF

There are rests and pauses in great music. There should be rests
and pauses in great living. There should be breaks in the day's
work. What does a break do? It breaks monotony. It breaks
tensions. It breaks frustrations. It breaks routine. It breaks
resistance. It breaks fatigue. Take a break for a fresh start.

WILFERD PETERSON

All work and no play makes Jack a dull boy.

UNKNOWN

Even youths grow tired and weary, and young men stumble
and fall; but those who hope in the Lord will renew their strength.
They will soar on wings like eagles; they will run and not grow
weary, they will walk and not be faint.

ISAIAH 40:30-31

The trail is the thing, not the end of the trail.
Travel too fast and you miss all you are traveling for.

LOUIS L'AMOUR, RIDE THE DARK TRAIL

To me, the garden is a doorway to other worlds; one of them, of
course, is the world of birds. The garden is their dinner table,
bursting with bugs and worms and succulent berries
(so plant more to accommodate you both).

ANNE RAVER

Learn to enjoy little things—there are so many of them.

UNKNOWN

Just as Jesus went to the garden
to reflect and pray,

So, too, should we gather our thoughts
in a quiet and humble way.

ROBERT J. HALL

Stop and smell the roses.

UNKNOWN

Stand in God's presence. Stand still and wait.
Sometimes that's all a soul can do. Too repentant to speak,
but too hopeful to leave. We just stand.

MAX LUCADO, HE STILL MOVES STONES

Prescription for a happier, healthier life: resolve to slow your pace;
learn to say no gracefully; resist the temptation to chase after more
pleasures, hobbies, and social entanglements. You must "hold the
line"…blocking out the intruders and defending the home team.

DR. JAMES DOBSON
WHAT WIVES WISH THEIR HUSBANDS KNEW ABOUT WOMEN

The lad had come home from school and dashed right back out of
the house. His mother called to him, "Where are you going?" The
son yelled back, "Out to play." "With those holes in your shoes?"
"No, with the kids across the street."

DOC BLAKELY

HONOR YOURSELF WITH DIGNITY

All over the world peoples are striving for a new and fuller
meaning of life. No challenge is more important than to give
concrete meaning to the idea of human dignity.

UNKNOWN

Where is there dignity unless there is honesty?

MARCUS TULLIUS CICERO (106-43 B.C.)

The friendships which last are those wherein each friend respects the
other's dignity to the point of not really wanting anything in return.

CYRIL CONNOLLY

A teenager is often desperately in need of
respect and dignity. Give him these gifts.

DR. JAMES DOBSON, THE STRONG-WILLED CHILD

Dignity of the common laborer
is the bedrock of creating national wealth.

ADAM SMITH, THE WEALTH OF NATIONS

The truly American sentiment recognizes the
dignity of labor and the fact that honor lies in honest toil.

GROVER CLEVELAND

In today's language it could be said
that a person with dignity is a "class act."

ROBERT J. HALL

She makes linen garments and sells them, and supplies the
merchants with sashes. She is clothed with strength and dignity;
she can laugh at the days to come. She speaks with wisdom, and
faithful instruction is on her tongue.

PROVERBS 31:24-26 NIV

Dignity is like a perfume; those who use it are scarcely conscious of it.

QUEEN CHRISTINA OF SWEDEN (1626-1689)

That man is a success who has lived well, laughed often, and
loved much; who has gained the respect of intelligent men and
the love of children; who has filled his niche and accomplished his
task; who leaves the world better than he found it,...who looked
for the best in others and gave the best he had.

ROBERT LOUIS STEVENSON

It is much more dignified to say we're moving in cycles rather than
running around in circles, although it comes to about the same thing.

THE PUBLIC SPEAKER'S TREASURE CHEST

The first thing in the human personality
that dissolves in alcohol is dignity.

UNKNOWN

MIND YOUR MANNERS

Manners are the happy way of doing things; each one a stroke of genius or of love—now repeated and hardened into usage.

RALPH WALDO EMERSON

Nothing is more reasonable and cheap than good manners.

ANONYMOUS

Some say I believe in old-fashioned traits: courtesy, politeness, and consideration. I do believe in these qualities, but they aren't old-fashioned. They never go out of style— even when they seem to be increasingly scarce.

COACH JOHN WOODEN

Hey, kids, here's a tip for you! If you want to get along well with Mom and Dad, always say such things as:

* Thank you   * Yes, Ma'am

* Please   * No, Ma'am

* You're welcome   * Yes, Sir

* Excuse me   * No, Sir

Also, write thank you notes to those who give you gifts.

ROBERT J. HALL

Good manners are a part of good morals; and it is
as much our duty as our interest to practice both.

JOHN HUNTER

Manners are a combination of behavior,
social custom, and being respectful of others.

UNKNOWN

The test of good manners is to be patient with bad ones.

SOLOMON IBN GABIROL

Use your heads as you live and work among outsiders.
Don't miss a trick. Make the most of every opportunity. Be
gracious in your speech. The goal is to bring out the best in others
in a conversation, not put them down, not cut them out.

COLOSSIANS 4:5-6, THE MESSAGE

All the education young men receive will be in vain
if they do not learn good manners.

MAHATMA GANDHI

When supper was served, Helen refused a second helping
of ice cream with a polite but wistful, "No, thank you!"

"Do have some more, dear!" her hostess urged.

"Mother told me to say, 'No, thank you,' " Helen explained
naively, "but I don't think she could have known how
small that first helping was going to be!"

THE PUBLIC SPEAKER'S TREASURE CHEST

Good Rules to Live By

From a 1909 religious publication comes a set of rules used in
London, England schools. These rules are timeless.

Courtesy to Yourself
Be honest, truthful, and pure.
Do not use bad language.
Keep your face and hands clean,
and your clothes and boots brushed and neat.
Keep out of bad company.

Courtesy at Home
Help your parents as much as you can.
Be kind to your brothers and sisters.
Do not be selfish, but share all your good things.
Do your best to please your parents.

Courtesy at School
Be respectful to your teachers, and help them as much as you can.
Observe the school rules.
Do not copy.
Do not cut the desks or write in the reading books.
Never let another be punished for your mistakes; that is cowardly.

Courtesy at Play
Do not cheat at games. Do not bully.
Be pleasant and not quarrelsome.

Do not jeer at or call your schoolmates by names
which they do not like.

Courtesy in the Street

Do not push or run against people.
Do not chalk on walls, doors, or gates.
Do not annoy shopkeepers by loitering at their shop.
Do not throw stones or destroy property.
Do not throw orange peels or make slides on the pavement; this
often results in dangerous accidents.
Do not make fun of old or crippled people.
Be courteous to strangers, but don't go with them.

Courtesy Everywhere

Remember to say "Please" and "Thank you."
Always mind your own business.
Before entering a room it is often courteous to knock at the door;
do not forget to close it after you.
Always show care, pity, and consideration for animals.
Never be rude to anybody, whether older or younger,
richer or poorer than yourself.
Always show attention to older people by opening the door for
them, bringing them what they require (hat, chair, etc.),
giving up your seat for them if necessary.
Never interrupt when a person is speaking.
Be tidy. Be punctual.

Compassion Comes From the Heart

Compassion—two hearts tugging at one load.

CHARLES H. PARKHURST

Blessed is he who has regard for the weak;
the Lord delivers him in times of trouble. The Lord will protect
him and preserve his life; He will bless him in the land and not
surrender him to the desire of his foes.

PSALMS 41:1-2

Being unwanted, unloved, uncared for, forgotten by everybody, I
think that is a much greater hunger, a much greater poverty than
the person who has nothing to eat...We must find each other.

MOTHER TERESA

When you are good to others, you are best to yourself.

BENJAMIN FRANKLIN

The value of compassion cannot be overemphasized.
Anyone can criticize. It takes a true believer to be compassionate.

ARTHUR H. STAINBACK

The dew of compassion is a tear.

GEORGE GORDON BYRON (LORD BYRON)

Compassion—your pain in my heart.

UNKNOWN

Compassion is that heartfelt instinct to help others in time of need.

ROBERT J. HALL

As a father has compassion on his children, so the Lord has compassion on those who fear him; for he knows how we are formed, he remembers that we are dust.

PSALMS 103:13-14

Man may dismiss compassion from his heart, but God will never.

WILLIAM COWPER

Nobody has ever measured, not even poets,
how much the heart can hold.

ZELDA FITZGERALD

It was one of the worst days of my life: the washing machine broke down, the telephone kept ringing, my head ached, and the mail carrier brought a bill I had no money to pay.

Almost to the breaking point, I lifted my one-year-old into his highchair, leaned my head against the tray, and began to cry.

Without a word, my son took his pacifier
out of his mouth and stuck it in mine.

CLARA NULL

We should all follow the advice of President Abraham Lincoln who said, "Let people be touched by the better angels of our nature."

SMILE! GIVE IT TO OTHERS

A smile is the whisper of a laugh.

UNKNOWN

Today, give a stranger one of your smiles.
It might be the only sunshine he sees all day.

MOM OF H. JACKSON BROWN

Most smiles are started by another smile.

UNKNOWN

A cheerful heart is good medicine,
but a crushed spirit dries up the bones.

PROVERBS 17:22

Thank you for the gifts you gave my life today.
You gave me a smile when I couldn't find one.

RICHARD FLINT

Smile—an inexpensive way to improve one's looks.

UNKNOWN

Let us always meet each other with a smile,
for the smile is the beginning of love.

MOTHER TERESA

Here's one thing money can't buy: a baby's smile.

UNKNOWN

For new parents a beautiful rainbow cannot produce the same sense of wonder and joy as their baby's first smile.

ROBERT J. HALL

A smile costs nothing, but gives much. It enriches those who receive, without making poorer those who give. It takes but a moment, but the memory of it sometimes lasts forever. None is so rich or mighty that he can get along without it, and none is so poor but that he can be made rich by it. A smile creates happiness in the home, fosters good will in business, and is the countersign of friendship. It brings rest to the weary, cheer to the discouraged, sunshine to the sad, and it is nature's best antidote for trouble.
Yet it cannot be bought, begged, borrowed, or stolen, for it is something that is of no value to anyone until it is given away. Some people are too tired to give you a smile. Give them one of yours, as none needs a smile so much as he who has no more to give.

UNKNOWN

Wrinkles should merely indicate where smiles have been.

SAMUEL LANGHORNE CLEMENS (MARK TWAIN)

Everybody should pay his taxes with a smile.
I tried it, but they wanted cash.

BRAUDE'S HANDBOOK OF HUMOR

Your Values Are the Real You

Mankind is not born with values. Values are learned
and adopted. Things we see, hear, and read help mold our values.
Always look for nothing but the best and most honorable
sources for guidance, especially the Bible.

ROBERT J. HALL

The Beatitudes

Blessed are the poor in spirit, for theirs is the kingdom of heaven.

Blessed are those who mourn, for they will be comforted.

Blessed are the meek, for they will inherit the earth.

Blessed are those who hunger and thirst for righteousness,
for they will be filled.

Blessed are the merciful, for they will be shown mercy.

Blessed are the pure in heart, for they will see God.

Blessed are the peacemakers, for they will be called sons of God.

Blessed are those who are persecuted because of righteousness,
for theirs is the kingdom of heaven.

MATTHEW 5:3-10 NIV

I know the plans I have for you, says the Lord. They are plans for
good and not for evil, to give you a future and a hope.

JEREMIAH 29:11 TLB

Something to Remember

You cannot bring about prosperity by discouraging thrift.

You cannot strengthen the weak by weakening the strong.

You cannot help little men by tearing down big men.

You cannot help the wage earner by pulling down the wage payer.

You cannot further brotherhood of man
by encouraging class hatred.

You cannot help the poor by destroying the rich.

You cannot establish sound security on borrowed money.

You cannot keep out of trouble by spending more than you earn.

You cannot build character and courage
by taking away men's initiative and independence.

You cannot help men permanently by doing for them
what they could and should do for themselves.

ABRAHAM LINCOLN

When the preacher's little daughter stumped her toe and said,
"Darn!" he reasoned with her: "Sweet, if you'll never say that word
again, I'll give you a dime."

A few days later she came to him and said, "Papa, I've got a word
now that's worth half a dollar."

LEROY BROWNLOW

OUR VALUES ARE OUR BELIEFS

On a plaque at Rockefeller Center in New York City is the following expression of the beliefs of John D. Rockefeller, Jr.:

I believe in the supreme worth of the individual and in his right to life, liberty and the pursuit of happiness.

I believe that every right implies a responsibility, every opportunity an obligation, every possession a duty.

I believe in the dignity of labor, whether with head or hand, that the world owes no man a living but that it owes every man an opportunity to make a living.

I believe that truth and justice are fundamental to an enduring social order.

I believe in the sacredness of a promise that a man's word should be as good as his bond, that character not wealth or power or position is of supreme worth.

I believe that the rendering of useful service is the common duty of mankind and that only in the purifying fire of sacrifice is the dross of selfishness consumed and the greatest of the human soul set free.

I believe in an all wise and loving God and that the individual's highest fulfillment, greatest happiness and widest usefulness are to be found in living in harmony with his will.

I believe that love is the greatest thing in the world, that it alone can overcome hate, that right can and will triumph over might.

THE EXECUTIVE SPEECHWRITER NEWSLETTER

The fear of the Lord is the beginning of wisdom,
and knowledge of the Holy One is understanding.

PROVERBS 9:10 NIV

A treasure chest full of silver and gold cannot compare
to good moral values such as honesty, character,
love and service to others, which come from the heart.

GRANDMA, MARY ANN HALL

Values are the building blocks upon which our lives are built and
through which we are known. As individuals, families and communi-
ties, we hand our values down from generation to generation, hoping
they will be preserved and honored as well as strengthened.

WEALTH OF WISDOM, A TREASURE OF BASIC VALUES

A partner with different values won't just pull you in
a different direction; he or she will pull you down.

GOD'S BEST FOR YOUR SUCCESS

Six-year-old Willie was lecturing little George, aged three, on the
value of various coins in his pocket. "Now, this," he said, "is a dime.
It will buy two candy bars. This is a nickel. It will buy only one candy
bar." He fished around and brought out a third coin. "And this," he
said, "is a penny. All it is good for is Sunday School."

BRAUDE'S HANDBOOK OF HUMOR

I think values are the most important thing you can teach
your children. If there's no values, there's nothing left.

UMED DUGAR

FAITH REACHES TOWARD GOD

Faith means being sure of the things we hope for. And faith
means knowing that something is real even if we do not see it.

HEBREWS 11:1 ICB

I believe the most valuable contribution a parent can
make to his child is to instill in him a genuine faith in God. What
greater ego satisfaction could there be than knowing that the
Creator of the universe is acquainted with me, personally? That he
understands my fears and anxieties; that his only Son, Jesus, gave
his life for me; that he can turn my liabilities into assets and my
emptiness into fullness; that a better life follows this one!
This is fulfillment at its richest!

DR. JAMES DOBSON, DR. DOBSON ANSWERS YOUR QUESTIONS
ABOUT CONFIDENT, HEALTHY FAMILIES

Faith is the daring of the soul to go farther than it can see.

WILLIAM NEWTON CLARKE

Faith is putting all your eggs in God's basket,
then counting your blessings before they hatch.

RAMONA C. CARROLL

Faith is like a kite. The harder the wind blows, the higher it goes.

M. L. PERRY

Faith is the wire that connects you to grace,
and over which grace comes streaming from God.

ANONYMOUS

Man must climb a ladder of faith to reach the
extended hand of God's mercy and grace.

ROBERT J. HALL

The principal part of faith is patience.

GEORGE MACDONALD, WEIGHED AND WANTING

Believers face the same pressures as unbelievers,
but they face them with faith instead of fear.

GOD'S BEST FOR YOUR SUCCESS

When evangelist Billy Graham was asked to give the
invocation at President Bush's inauguration, he cited this
quotation by George Washington: "America stands on two great
pillars—faith and morality. Without these, our foundation
crumbles." Faith is like love: It cannot be forced.

"This morning," said the minister, "I'm going to
speak on the relationship between fact and faith. It is a fact that
you are sitting here in the sanctuary. It is also a fact that I am
standing here speaking. But it is faith that makes me believe
that you might be listening to what I have to say."

EXECUTIVE SPEECHWRITER'S NEWSLETTER

ENTHUSIASM WORKS WONDERS

Enthusiasm is like a freshly perked pot of morning coffee.
It shouts, "Good morning, world, here I come! Either get on
the bandwagon or kindly step out of the way because
I've got things to do an' time's awastin'!"

ROBERT J. HALL

The great accomplishments of man have resulted
from the transmission of ideas and enthusiasm.

THOMAS J. WATSON, FOUNDER OF IBM

Every great and commanding movement in the
annals of the world is the triumph of enthusiasm.
Nothing great was ever achieved without it.

RALPH WALDO EMERSON

Regardless of whether you're leading as a teacher,
coach, parent, or businessperson, or you're a member of a leadership team, you must have enthusiasm. Without it you cannot be
industrious to the full level of your ability. With it you stimulate
others to higher and higher levels of achievement.

COACH JOHN WOODEN

Enthusiasm is unmistakable evidence
that you're in love with your work.

UNKNOWN

We act as though comfort and luxury were the
chief requirements of life, when all that we need to make us
really happy is something to be enthusiastic about.

CHARLES KINGSLEY

Every man is enthusiastic at times. One man has enthusiasm
for thirty minutes—another man has it for thirty days, but it is
the man who has it for thirty years who makes a success in life.

EDWARD B. BUTLER

Enthusiasm is the vibrant thrill in your voice that sways the wills
of others into harmony with your own. Enthusiasm is a magnet
that draws kindred souls with irresistible force and electrifies them
with the magnetism of its own resolves.

PRESBYTERIAN OF THE SOUTH

Enthusiasm is the best protection in any situation.
Wholeheartedness is contagious. Give yourself,
if you wish to get others.

DAVID SEABURY

If you can give your son only one gift, let it be enthusiasm.

BRUCE BARTON

It's really a thrill when our kids come home from
summer camp. Enthusiastically they yell, "Eureka! Eureka!"
and they really do. They haven't had a bath in weeks.

ROBERT ORBEN

KEEP A GOOD CONSCIENCE

If a person does what he thinks is right, that something within
him called conscience approves and, in so doing, gives him a
feeling of self-respect and peace. But if he knowingly does wrong,
there is that internal witness which blames and tortures him.

LEROY BROWNLOW

Conscience is God's presence in man.

EMMANUAL SWEDENBORG, 18TH-CENTURY PHILOSOPHER

There is no pillow so soft as a clear conscience.

FRENCH PROVERB

Conscience is e-mail your head gets from Heaven.

BILL KEANE, THE FAMILY CIRCUS

A good digestion depends upon a good conscience.

BENJAMIN DISRAELI

Conscience is merely our own judgment of the right
or wrong of our actions, and so can never be a safe guide
unless enlightened by the word of God.

TRYON EDWARDS

So I strive always to keep my conscience clear before God and man.

APOSTLE PAUL, ACTS 24:16

Conscience is the little bird that says,
"No! No! No!" when you are tempted to do wrong.

Robert J. Hall

Conscience warns us as a friend before it punishes as a judge.

Stanislas I Leszcyski

Our conscience was designed by God to guide us in
making moral and ethical decisions. Within our conscience God
placed a sense of oughtness, the ability to know right from wrong.
He did not, however, leave it at that. He also made it possible for
us to train and develop our conscience. That training can
either make us Christ centered or flesh centered.

Dr. Hillery Motsinger

One of the most necessary conditions of happy living
and sound health is an untroubled conscience. Happiness comes
through the feeling of peace: peace with one's self, peace
with one's record and peace with one's God.

Leroy Brownlow

The one thing that doesn't abide by majority rule
is a person's conscience.

Harper Lee, author

Small boy's definition of conscience: "Something that makes you
tell your mother before your sister does."

National Motorist

BEWARE OF A GUILTY CONSCIENCE

Just because our conscience tells us that something we want to
do is right or wrong, does not mean that we will follow its advice.
Sometimes, we will ignore it and go against its advice.
This creates what we commonly call a guilty conscience.

DR. HILLERY MOTSINGER

Fire such as martyrs felt at the stake were but a plaything
compared with the flames of a burning conscience.
Thunderbolts and tornadoes are nothing in force
compared with the charges of a guilty conscience.

CHARLES H. SPURGEON

There is no witness so terrible—no accuser
so powerful as conscience which dwells within us.

SOPHOCLES

The guilty conscience makes cowards and defeatists of
all persons. The smitten conscience fears and dreads without real
cause. The person with a fearful conscience is so afraid that he sees
his shadow as a stalking enemy to destroy him; every kitten as a
lion to devour him; every bush as a tree from which he
may hang; and every hill as an unclimbable mountain.

LEROY BROWNLOW

It is astonishing how soon the whole conscience begins
to unravel if a single stitch drops. One single sin indulged
in makes a hole you could put your head through.

CHARLES BUXTON

And when a person knows the right thing to do,
but does not do it, then he is sinning.

JAMES 4:17 ICB

A guilty conscience is like a smashed thumbnail;
it tells you very clearly to never do that again.

ROBERT J. HALL

A guilty conscience lashes the soul as the waves do the shore, with
all the unrest and turbulence of the splashing breakers. Thus
conscience has the power to make us happy or unhappy, well or sick.

LEROY BROWNLOW

My guilt has overwhelmed me. Like a load it weighs me down.

PSALMS 38:4 ICB

Conscience is the inner voice that warns us
that someone may be looking.

H. L. MENCKEN

Two fellows, fishing on a Sunday morning, were feeling pretty guilty.
Said one to the other: "I suppose we should have stayed home and
gone to church." To which the second angler replied lazily, "Heck, I
couldn't have gone to church anyway. My wife's sick in bed."

BRAUDE'S HANDBOOK OF HUMOR

SUFFERING MAKES YOU STRONG

Suffering can do good things for us:

A. To give us wisdom (through experience)
B. To give us hope and endurance
C. To make us humble
D. To chasten us like a father disciplines his son
E. To keep us from becoming too attached to this world.

UNKNOWN

And we also have joy with our troubles because we
know that these troubles produce patience. And patience
produces character, and character produces hope.

ROMANS 5:3-4 ICB

Life is teaching you some painful lessons.
But it is from adversity that strength is born. You may have
lost the inning, but I know you'll win the game.

MOM OF H. JACKSON BROWN

The gem cannot be polished without friction,
nor man perfected without trials.

CONFUCIUS

The way I see it, if you want the rainbow,
you gotta put up with the rain.

DOLLY PARTON

Every time you get knocked down you get up stronger.

MARLON BRANDO, ACTOR

Christ gives us inner strength to handle both prosperity and adversity.

GOD'S BEST FOR YOUR SUCCESS

Some struggles are self-imposed like the training of
an Olympic athlete. Other struggles come without warning
as a result of time and chance. These struggles can be endured
and overcome with the help of the Lord.

ROBERT J. HALL

So that you and I would believe that the Healer knows our hurts,
He voluntarily became one of us. He placed himself in our
position. He suffered our pains and felt our fears.

MAX LUCADO

Worry does not empty tomorrow of its sorrow;
it empties today of its strength.

CORRIE TEN BOOM

I can do all things through Christ who strengthens me.

PHILIPPIANS 4:13

About half your troubles come from wanting
your way. The other half comes from getting it.

THE COWBOY'S LOGIC

Some persons won't suffer in silence because
that would take the pleasure out of it.

BOB PHILLIPS

KIDS SAY THE FUNNIEST THINGS

A naughty little girl was put in a clothes closet
for punishment. For 15 minutes there wasn't a sound. Finally the
stern, but anxious mother opened the door and peered inside.

"What are you doing in there?" she asked.

From the darkness came the emphatic answer. "I'm thpittin' on
your new hat, I'm thpittin' on your new dreth, I'm thpittin' on your
new thatin thlippers and—and—."There was a breathless pause.

"And what!" cried the mother.

Came the voice of vengeance, "Now I'm waitin' for more thpit!"

UNKNOWN

A young child in church for the first time watched the ushers pass the
offering plates. When they neared her pew, the youngster said to her
father, "Remember, you don't have to pay for me, Dad. I'm under five."

UNKNOWN

Let the little children come to me. Don't stop them, because the
kingdom of heaven belongs to people who are like these children.

MATTHEW 19:14 ICB

When your dad is mad and asks you,
"Do I look stupid?" don't answer him.

HEATHER, AGE 16

Three-year-old Bobby didn't like the routine
of being scrubbed, especially when soap was applied. "Bobby,
don't you want to be nice and clean?" his mother asked. "Sure,"
replied Bobby, "but can't you just dust me?"

UNKNOWN

I broke and dropped six raw eggs in a mixing bowl. Before I beat
them, Stuart (age 3), climbed on a chair and saw the six round,
golden egg yolks and said, "Mama, who put peaches in our eggs?"

MARY ANN HALL, GRANDMA

It reminds me of the little kid who, just as he was being
handed his report card, said, "Teacher, I think somebody should
warn you, my Dad says that unless my math grades go up,
somebody's gonna get a whipping."

BERNARD RANDOLPH, COMMANDER AIR FORCE SYSTEMS COMMAND

Wear a hat when feeding seagulls.

ROCKY, AGE 9

Remember you're never too old to hold your father's hand.

MOLLY, AGE 11

Remember the two places you are always welcome—
church and grandma's house.

JOANNE, AGE 11

Never try to baptize a cat.

LAURA, AGE 13

YOUTH—AND THIS, TOO, SHALL PASS

A teacher tells of a first-grade class that was being particularly unruly. Finally she slammed a ruler down on her desk and said, in a loud voice, "I'm tired of this children. Do you hear me, I'm tired. I'm tired of telling you to be quiet and I'm tired of telling you to sit down and I'm tired of telling you to pay attention to what you're doing. I'm tired of it, children, I'm tired of it. "There were several moments of silence before one little girl raised her hand and suggested, "Then why don't you go take a nice little nap?"

DOC BLAKELY

I figured out why teenagers grow so fast—It's all that fast food.

UNKNOWN

Have you ever gone into a teenager's room?
They're all done in a very interesting style—Early Slob!

ROBERT ORBEN

Train up a child in the way he should go:
and when he is old, he will not depart from it.

PROVERBS 22:6 KJV

The struggles of youth produce experiences
and wisdom which lead to great things later in life.

ROBERT J. HALL

Children are like clocks; they must be allowed to run.

DR. JAMES DOBSON

I heard about a teenage girl talking to her father
about all of her problems. She told him of the terrible peer
pressure she faced, about conflicts with friends, and difficulties
with school work and teachers. In an attempt to help her put
everything in perspective, he told her that life was not as dark as it
might seem and, in fact, much of her worry was perhaps unneces-
sary. "That's easy for you to say, Dad," the daughter replied.
"You already have all your problems over with."

UNKNOWN

Youth is the opportunity to do something and to become somebody.

THEODORE THORNTON MUNGER

Salute To Youth

You are the hope of the world.
You are radiant with energy.
You are undaunted by impossibilities.
You accept the challenge of today.
You face life as a great adventure.
You dream noble dreams.

Your marching feet beat a symphony of progress.
As you march into the future with banners flying,
Eyes shining with the splendor of your ideals,
We proudly stand at salute,
For you are the hope of the world.

WILFERD PETERSON

Master Your Anger

He who conquers his anger has conquered an enemy.

GERMAN PROVERB

Anger is a neutral feeling that is neither good nor bad;
it is the expression of anger that may be sinful.

DR. HILLERY MOTSINGER

Anger is just one letter short of Danger.

ELEANOR DOAN

Anger can be spiritually fatal. It shrivels the soul.

MAX LUCADO

When you are angry, do not sin. And do not go on being
angry all day. Do not give the devil a way to defeat you.

EPHESIANS 4:26-27 ICB

He best keeps from anger who remembers that
God is always looking upon him.

PLATO

If you find yourself growing angry at someone,
pray for him—anger cannot live in an atmosphere of prayer.

W. T. McELROY

The anger of the prudent never shows.

BURMESE PROVERB

Anger is the only thing to put off till tomorrow.

Slovakian Proverb

Anger is a poor leader to follow.

Robert J. Hall

If you are patient in one moment of anger,
you will escape a hundred days of sorrow.

Chinese Proverb

Angry words! O let them never from my tongue unbridled slip;
may the heart's best impulse ever check them ere they soil the lip.

Sunday School Teacher, 1867

When you are angry or frustrated, what comes out?
Whatever it is, it's a good indication of what you're made of.

Mom of H. Jackson Brown

When angry, count ten before you speak;
if very angry, count a hundred.

Thomas Jefferson

My recipe for dealing with anger and frustration: set the
kitchen timer for 20 minutes, cry, rant and rave, and at the sound
of the bell, simmer down and go about 'business as usual'.

Phyllis Diller

A lady bent a fender on their new car and a neighbor asked if
her husband got mad. "He didn't say much," said the wife. "But his
boss said the smoke alarm went off when he got to work."

Doc Blakely

GAMBLING IS VERY UNWISE

Gambling is a bad bet! It violates every principle of honesty, work, responsibility, and stewardship in the Bible. It is a scourge and blight upon America, and it has no place in the life of the Christian.

CLARENCE DeLOACH ANGLETON ACCENTS

Gambling is the child of avarice,
the brother of iniquity, and the father of mischief.

GEORGE WASHINGTON

Gambling isn't a gamble. It's a sure thing. You lose.

ANDY ROONEY

Those who want to become rich bring temptation to themselves. They are caught in a trap. They begin to want many foolish things that will hurt them, things that ruin and destroy people. The love of money causes all kinds of evil. Some people have left the true faith because they want to get more and more money. But they have caused themselves much sorrow.

I TIMOTHY 6:9-10 ICB

Gambling of any kind separates us from God and leads
to the worship of the idols of luck, chance and greed.

REX M. RODGERS, SEDUCING AMERICA

Gambling: The sure way of getting nothing for something.

WILSON MIZNER

Just as the wood ducklings learn to heed their
mother's warnings of danger, so too, shall you heed
the warnings of your parents against gambling.

ROBERT J. HALL

I dare to say that there is no sin that does more
swiftly send men down to hell than gambling.

CHARLES SPURGEON

Walk away from get-rich-quick schemes.
One mistake can cause years of financial agony,
along with a severe strain on your marriage.

MICHAEL MATTHEWS

Gambling destroys marriages, underminds
the work ethic, increases crime, motivates suicide,
destroys the financial security of families.....

DR. JAMES DOBSON, FAMILY NEWS

Gambling causes some men and women to use the
family's food, clothing, utility and medical money on their
"hobby," A man must provide for his house. (I Timothy 5:8)

UNKNOWN

In Las Vegas, money can be lost in more ways than won, yet most
of us have two chances of becoming wealthy—slim and none.

DOC BLAKELY

ALL FORMS OF GAMBLING ARE BAD

Experts tell us that gambling addiction is related to several factors, chief among these being access to gambling and the speed of the games. Internet gambling is a lethal combination of these factors.

JAMES C. DOBSON, PH.D.

The lottery is no good. It robs from the poor.
It robs from my neighbors. People lose a lot of money.
The government has no business being involved.

SELLER OF LOTTERY TICKETS IN MASSACHUSETTS

Even if some forms of gambling are legal, such as the lottery, it is an unwise risk-taking that most often hurts the young and the poor.

ROBERT J. HALL

So anyone who thinks he is standing strong should be careful not to fall. The only temptations that you have are the temptations that all people have. But you can trust God. He will not let you be tempted more than you can stand. But when you are tempted, God will also give you a way to escape that temptation.

I CORINTHIANS 10:12-13 ICB

Every light, every gambling casino and every hotel in
Las Vegas were bought and paid for by the losses of gamblers.

JOHN W. SMITH

The U.S. Postal Service is clamping down on chain letters—
schemes that involve sending money to a name on a list.
Such illegal schemes are regarded as gambling.

THE KIPLINGER WASHINGTON LETTER, APRIL 30, 1999

The soldiers at the foot of the cross threw dice for my Savior's
garments. And I have never heard the rattling of dice but I have
conjured up the dreadful scene of Christ on his cross, and gamblers
at the foot of it, with their dice bespattered with his blood.

CHARLES H. SPURGEON

There is nothing that wears out a fine face like the vigils of
the card-table. Hollow eyes, haggard looks, and pale complexions
are the natural indications of a female gamester.

SIR RICHARD STEELE

It always bothers me to put a silver dollar in a slot machine and
then pull the handle down. It's the same motion you use to flush.

ROBERT ORBEN

Hear about the tourist vacationing in Las Vegas?
He didn't have any money to gamble so he just watched the games
and bet mentally. In no time at all, he'd lost his mind.

DOC BLAKELY

Gambling: That's throwing away money
while other people cheer you on.

UNKNOWN

COMMITMENT REVEALS CHARACTER

Make important decisions only once and escape the necessity
of rehashing them again and again. These are usually decisions
on how we are going to live. For example, we will decide to be
honest, to be on time, and to go to church on Sunday.
We make commitments carefully, then keep them.

MAMIE McCULLOUGH

Let your handshake be as binding as a signed contract.

H. JACKSON BROWN

Is life so dear, or peace so sweet, as to be purchased at the price of
chains and slavery? Forbid it, Almighty God! I know not what course
others may take, but as for me, give me liberty, or give me death.

PATRICK HENRY
SPEECH IN THE VIRGINIA CONVENTION, 1775

You don't start a business venture without proper planning—and
you don't follow Christ without a wholehearted commitment.

GOD'S BEST FOR YOUR SUCCESS

Every brave man is a man of his word.

PIERRE CORNEILLE

He who is most slow in making a commitment
is the most faithful in its performance.

JEAN JACQUES ROUSSEAU

Love is not defined by the highs and lows,
but is dependent on a commitment of the will.

DR. JAMES DOBSON
WHAT WIVES WISH THEIR HUSBANDS KNEW ABOUT WOMEN

Remember—Your promise, your commitment
to marriage is for a lifetime.

ROBERT J. HALL

Jesus said, "Anyone who begins to plow a field
but keeps looking back is of no use in the kingdom of God."

LUKE 9:62 ICB

Above all keep yourselves pure and clean,
and learn to keep your promises even at the cost of life.

MOHANDAS KARAMCHAND (MAHATMA) GANDHI

A commitment is a debt you should not forget.

PHILIPPINE PROVERB

It's like the story of the chicken and the pig who were walking
down the road together when they saw a sign in a restaurant
advertising ham and eggs. The chicken said, "Look, isn't that
nice? Together you and I are the most popular items for people's
breakfast." The pig replied, "Yes, but for you it's only
a part-time job. For me it's a total commitment."

UNKNOWN

Discipline is Rewarded

Discipline may seem harsh at the moment, but the ultimate goal is to teach self-discipline for later in life.

ROBERT J. HALL

The only discipline that lasts is self-discipline.

BUM PHILLIPS, FORMER HOUSTON OILERS HEAD COACH

You will never be the person you can be if pressure, tension and discipline are taken out of your life.

DR. JAMES BILKEY

If a person does not punish his children, he does not love them. But the person who loves his children is careful to correct them.

PROVERBS 13:24 ICB

The hardest blow that God ever laid upon his child was inflicted by the hand of love.

DR. CHARLES H. SPURGEON

Children thrive best in an atmosphere of genuine love, undergirded by reasonable, consistent discipline.

DR. JAMES DOBSON, DARE TO DISCIPLINE

Psychiatrists tell us that discipline doesn't break a child's spirit half as often as the lack of it breaks a parent's heart.

UNKNOWN

Lovers of freedom often overlook this paradox:
There is no true freedom without discipline. An ordered and
disciplined life gives us freedom to do the things we want to do....
Life offers a choice between self-discipline and imposed discipline.
Discipline is essential. Have it we must, whether we like it or not.

THE PUBLIC SPEAKER'S TREASURE CHEST

The handwriting on the wall usually means
someone's going to get a spanking.

SPEAKER'S SOURCEBOOK

Parental warmth after punishment is essential
to demonstrate to the child that it was his behavior,
and not the child himself, that the parent rejected.

DR. JAMES DOBSON, DARE TO DISCIPLINE

Discipline in schools is a problem these days.
Teaching today is like jungle warfare with lesson plans.

DOC BLAKELY

Discipline is what you inflict on one end of
a child to impress the other.

UNKNOWN

Teacher: "This is the fifth time this week that I have
had to punish you. What have you to say, Charles?"

Charles: "I'm glad it's Friday!"

SPEAKER'S SOURCEBOOK

BE NOT A FOOL

If 50 million people say a foolish thing, it is still a foolish thing.

ANATOLE FRANCE
FRENCH AUTHOR (1844-1924)

A foolish son brings grief to his father
and bitterness to the one who bore him.

PROVERBS 17:25

Former Congressman Brooks Hays told of a bishop who advised a politician to go out into the rain and lift his head heavenward. "It will bring a revelation to you." Next day the politician reported, "I followed your advice and no revelation came. The water poured down my neck and I felt like a fool." "Well," said the bishop, "isn't that quite a revelation for the first try?"

WOODEN BARREL

It is never wise to argue with a fool.
Bystanders don't know which is which.

SPEAKER'S SOURCEBOOK

You can always tell a real friend: When you've made a fool of yourself, he doesn't feel you've done a permanent job.

DR. LAURENCE J. PETER

We must learn to live together as brothers or perish together as fools.

MARTIN LUTHER KING, JR.

In seeking wisdom thou art wise;
in imagining that thou has attained it thou art a fool.

SIMON BEN AZZAI

It's easy to fool other people. Fooling yourself is a little harder.
Fooling God is impossible.

CHRIS HARRISON

The butcher was busy waiting on a customer when a woman
rushed in and said, "Give me a pound of cat food, quick!" Turning
to the other customer, who had been waiting for some time, said:
"I hope you don't mind my getting waited on before you."
"Not if you're that hungry," replied the other woman.

JACOB M. BRAUDE

The Grand Canyon is, of course, altogether valueless.
Ours has been the first, and doubtless to be the last,
party of Whites to visit this profitless locality.

LT. JOSEPH IVES
U.S. CORPS OF ENGINEERS, 1861

The customer in the New Orleans restaurant was loud and rude.
"What do you have to do to get a glass of water around this
dump?" A little old lady at the next table leaned over and said
sweetly, "Why not try setting yourself on fire?

DOC BLAKELY

Count Your Many Blessings

Not only count your blessings, but consider their source.

ETERNITY

The great inventor Thomas Edison once shocked his friends
by saying his deafness was his greatest blessing
because it saved him from the trouble of having to listen to
negative comments on why things couldn't be done.

UNKNOWN

Ask God's blessing for your work, but don't ask him to do it for you.

DAME FLORA ROBSO

To get the blessing we must do the work.

UNKNOWN

Some people are like land that gets plenty of rain. The land produces a
good crop for those who work it, and it receives God's blessings.

HEBREWS 6:7 ICB

Blessed is the man who is too busy to worry
in the daytime and too sleepy to worry at night.

UNKNOWN

It is sad, but too often our blessings are not
fully appreciated until we lose them.

ROBERT J. HALL

There are three requisites to the proper enjoyment of earthly
blessings: a thankful reflection on the goodness of the giver; a
deep sense of our own unworthiness; and a recollection of the
uncertainty of our long possessing them. The first will make us
grateful; the second, humble; and the third, moderate.

HANNAH MORE

The private and personal blessings we enjoy,
the blessings of immunity, safeguard, liberty, and integrity,
deserve the thanksgiving of a whole life.

JEREMY TAYLOR

Blessed are those who give without remembering
and take without forgetting.

ELIZABETH BIBESCO

May the Lord bless you and keep you.
May the Lord show you his kindness. May he have mercy on you.
May the Lord watch over you and give you peace.

NUMBERS 6:24-26

Before we sat down to our Thanksgiving dinner,
my wife spoke of our many blessings. First on her list came our six
healthy children. An hour later when we were at the table,
all was pandemonium. Noticing that my wife's eyes were closed,
I asked her what was the matter. "Nothing," she said,
"I am just praying for patience to endure my blessings.

E. C. STEVENSON

ALWAYS BE THANKFUL

Thanksgiving is good, thanksliving is better.

ELEANOR DOAN

Say So

Does a neighbor help a little,
As along the way you go—
Help to make your burden lighter?
Then why not tell him so!

Does a handclasp seem to lift you
From the depth of grief and woe,
When an old friend shares your sorrow?
Then why not tell him so!

Does your Heavenly Father give you
Many blessings here below?
Then on bended knee before Him
Frankly, gladly, tell Him so!

GERALDINE SEARFOSS

O Lord, that lends me life, lend me a heart replete with thankfulness.

WILLIAM SHAKESPEARE: HENRY VI, PART II

So then, just as you received Christ Jesus as Lord, continue to live
in him, rooted and built up in him, strengthened in the faith as
you were taught, and overflowing with thankfulness.

COLOSSIANS 2:6-7 NIV

Without Thy sunshine and Thy rain
We could not have the golden grain;
Without Thy love we'd not be fed;
We thank Thee for our daily bread.

ANONYMOUS

When I find a great deal of gratitude in a poor man, I take it
for granted there would be as much generosity if he were rich.

ALEXANDER POPE

Gratitude is the memory of the heart.

UNKNOWN

If you have nothing to be thankful for,
make up your mind that there is something wrong with you.

UNKNOWN

Pride slays thanksgiving, but an humble mind is the soil out of
which thanks naturally grow. A proud man is seldom a grateful
man, for he never thinks he gets as much as he deserves.

HENRY WARD BEECHER

The worship most acceptable to God
comes from a thankful and cheerful heart.

PLUTARCH

When the Sunday school teacher asked her class what they were
thankful for, one little fellow replied, "My glasses." He explained,
"They keep the boys from fighting me and the girls from kissing me."

TOGETHER

Thanksgiving is Special

The first Thanksgiving Proclamation was made by Governor Bradford three years after the Pilgrims settled at Plymouth:

To all Pilgrims

Inasmuch as the Father has given us an abundant harvest of Indian corn, wheat, peas, beans, squashes, and garden vegetables, and has made the forests to abound with game and the sea with fish, and inasmuch as he has protected us from the savages, has spared us from pestilence and disease, has granted us freedom to worship God according to our own conscience; now I, your magistrate, do proclaim that all Pilgrims do gather at the meeting house, between the hours of 9 and 12 in the day time, on Thursday, November 29, 1623, and the third year since the Pilgrims landed on Pilgrim Rock, there to listen to the pastor and render thanksgiving to the Almighty God for all his blessings.

WILLIAM BRADFORD, GOVERNOR OF THE COLONY

Be joyful always; pray continually; give thanks in all circumstances, for this is God's will for you in Christ Jesus.

I THESSALONIANS 5:16-18 NIV

O God, Thou hast given so much to us,
give one thing more—a grateful heart.

AMEN. GEORGE HERBERT

A thankful heart is not only the greatest virtue,
but the parent of all other virtues.

CICERO

One way God sets humans apart from other living
creatures is that mankind was given the ability to recognize
blessings and be thankful for them.

ROBERT J. HALL

Thanksgiving is nothing if not a glad and reverent lifting
of the heart to God in honour and praise for His goodness.

JAMES R. MILLER

If you have good health, unimpaired eyesight,
clear mental faculties and full use of all your limbs,
you have the four greatest causes of thankfulness in this world.
These are four great corner-stone blessings.

I.Q.M.

God has two dwellings: one in heaven
and the other in an open and thankful heart.

UNKNOWN

Last year we let the kids make Thanksgiving dinner and it really
brought home how unimaginative my wife and I have been all these
years. Not once have we ever thought of using Twinkies for stuffing.

ROBERT ORBEN

CONQUER YOUR FEARS

Don't permit fear of failure to prevent effort. We are all imperfect and will fail on occasions, but fear of failure is the greatest failure of all.

COACH JOHN WOODEN

The one battle most people lose is
the battle over the fear of failure...try...start...begin...
and you'll be assured you won the first round.

ROBERT H. SCHULLER

Some say if only my fears and doubts will leave then
I will get to work. But instead you should get to work
and then your fears and doubts will leave.

D. L. MOODY

The only thing we have to fear is fear itself.

FRANKLIN D. ROOSEVELT, 1933

Never fear shadows. They simply mean
there's a light shining somewhere nearby.

RUTH E. RENKEL

There are very few monsters who warrant the fear we have of them.

ANDRE GIDE, FRENCH AUTHOR/CRITIC (1869-1951)

I sought the Lord, and He heard me,
and delivered me from all my fears.

PSALMS 34:4 ICB

Even if I walk through a very dark valley, I will not be afraid because you are with me. Your rod and your walking stick comfort me.

PSALMS 23:4 ICB

Just as a weasel with fearless courage attacks
and kills a king snake to protect his family, so, too, shall you
overcome fear and defend your family when in danger.

ROBERT J. HALL

Fear can't be evaded. And it can't be avoided. It has to be met head on. If you're not willing to go to the heart of what it is you are afraid of, that fear will haunt you constantly. President Theodore Roosevelt once said, "I have often been afraid, but I wouldn't give in to it. I made myself act as though I was not afraid, and gradually my fear disappeared." Action is the only answer.

UNKNOWN

Worry is a thin stream of fear trickling through the mind. If encouraged, it cuts a channel into which all other thoughts are drained.

A. S. ROCHE

Jimmy: "Aw, you're afraid to fight."

Johnny: "Naw, I'm not, but if I fight
my mom'll find out and spank me."

Jimmy: "How'll she find out?"

Johnny: "She'll see the doctor going into your place."

BRAUDE'S HANDBOOK OF HUMOR

EXERCISE TO BE HEALTHY

High energy is almost always present in successful people.
Among other positive results, high energy permits you to hold
your course to success when things get tough. My best idea
for increasing energy is to eat more fruits and veggies,
eat less fat, and get on a reasonable program of exercise.

MAMIE MCCULLOUGH

I wish above all things that thou mayest prosper
and be in health, even as thy soul prospereth.

III JOHN 2

Children stand to benefit most of all, by learning
early in life to avoid eating and living patterns that may
lead to premature heart disease in adulthood.

CONTROL HIGH BLOOD PRESSURE

DON'T SMOKE CIGARETTES

REDUCE IF OVERWEIGHT

EAT FOODS LOW IN FAT AND CHOLESTEROL

HAVE REGULAR MEDICAL CHECK-UPS

EXERCISE MODERATELY EACH DAY

CONTROL DIABETES

VISADOR CLASSIC LINES

The best form of spiritual exercise is to
touch the floor regularly with your knees.

ANONYMOUS

I jogged for over 20 years. The greatest thing I learned was
the value of drinking plenty of water (H_2O). It rehydrates your
body after a sweaty workout. It is the "grease" that helps your
digestion, it reduces heartburn and it allows all your body parts to
work as they are designed. To a jogger ample water is a must.

ROBERT J. HALL

Why do I run? Tain't no mystery.
Wanna have a good medical history.
Doctor told me running is great, helps my blood cells circulate.

Great for the lungs, great for the ticker.
Can't nothin' getcha in better shape quicker.
Feels so healthy, feels so sweet
Pumpin' my arms and flappin' my feet.
Moldin' my muscles, firmin' my form,
Pantin' like a pack mule, sweatin' up a storm.

Keeps me youthful, keeps me loose,
Tightens my tummy and shrinks my caboose.
Beats bein' sluggish. Beats bein' lazy.
Why do I run? Maybe I'm crazy.

ED CUNNINGHAM

There's something wrong with the health club I joined.
The floors are so low I can't touch my toes.

GARY APPLE

PREPARATION COMES FIRST

Preparedness is the key to success and victory.

DOUGLAS MACARTHUR, U.S. MILITARY GENERAL

Winning is the science of preparation and preparation can be defined in three words. "Leave nothing undone. "No detail is too small. No task is too large. Most of the time, the difference between winning and losing, success and failure, can be the smallest detail or as they say in baseball, just a matter of inches.

REGGIE JACKSON
MAJOR LEAGUE OUTFIELDER AND SPORTS BROADCASTER

Seventy-five percent of the victory depends on preparation.

DR. C. E. MATTHEWS

By failing to prepare you are preparing to fail.

BENJAMIN FRANKLIN

The time will come when winter will ask
what you were doing all summer.

HENRY CLAY, AMERICAN STATESMAN

Ants are not very strong. But they store up food in the summer.

PROVERBS 30:25 ICB

You can give most things away. Power to you.
You cannot give away preparation.

CHARLES HODGE

I've never run a bad race when my training
has gone well. If I train well, I'll run well.

ALBERTO SALAZAR, DISTANCE RUNNER

Jesus prepared to select his disciples by
spending a night in prayer to God. You should always
pray to God before making important decisions.

ROBERT J. HALL

If people knew how hard I have had to work
to gain my mastery, it wouldn't seem wonderful at all.

MICHELANGELO, ITALIAN PAINTER/SCULPTOR

Victory does not come from the will to win, but the will to prepare.

COACH BUD WILKINSON

The time to prepare isn't after you have been given the
opportunity. It's long before that opportunity arises.
Once the opportunity arrives, it's too late to prepare.

COACH JOHN WOODEN

Whether you're trying to excel in athletics or any other field,
always practice. Look, listen, learn—and practice, practice,
practice. There is no substitute for work, no short cuts to the top.

FRANK ROBINSON
MAJOR LEAGUE OUTFIELDER AND MANAGER

Two little girls were discussing their families. "Why does
your grandmother read the Bible so much?" asked one. Replied
the other: "I think she's cramming for her finals."

BRAUDE'S HANDBOOK OF HUMOR

GOOFS WILL HAPPEN

As baseball legend Yogi Berra once said about his team:
"We made too many wrong mistakes."

In a University of Hawaii game a happy halfback
named Hilo leaped so high to catch a pass that the strain
broke the lacings on his pants. Six steps later the pants dropped
around his ankles. But Hilo stiff-armed one would-be tackler
and hippety-hopped ten yards for his touchdown.

OREN ARNOLD

I have a theory that the only original things we ever do are mistakes.

BILLY JOEL, SONGWRITER

Mistakes are the dues one pays for a full life.

SOPHIA LOREN, ITALIAN ACTRESS

Experience: The name we give our mistakes.

BOB PHILLIPS

If you don't learn anything from your mistakes
there's no sense in making them.

UNKNOWN

God, you know what I have done wrong.
I cannot hide my guilt from you.

PSALMS 69:5 ICB

An admission of error is a sign of strength rather than a weakness.

UNKNOWN

A man of genius makes no mistakes.
His errors are the portals of discovery.

JAMES JOYCE

No man ever became great except through many and great mistakes.

WILLIAM E. GLADSTONE

My favorite saying: "Remember your mistakes
just long enough to profit by them."

WILLIAM BRITTON

It is strange the way other people do not profit
when we point out their mistakes.

UNKNOWN

There is a story told about a minister who was late for
church on a Sunday that he was scheduled to give a very
important sermon. Driving to church, he was pulled over for
speeding by a traffic cop. As the officer was making out the ticket,
the minister looked up at him pleading, "In the words of the Bible,
'Blessed are the merciful, for they shall obtain mercy.'" The cop
looked at the minister, handed him a speeding ticket and replied,
"In the words of the Bible, 'Go thou and sin no more.'"

EXECUTIVE SPEECHWRITER NEWSLETTER

Architects cover their mistakes with ivy,
doctors with sod, and brides with mayonnaise.

BRAUDE'S HANDBOOK OF HUMOR

Be a Good Influence

Blessed is the influence of one true, loving human soul on another.

GEORGE ELIOT

All those young people who have a full life ahead of them should be noble and generous so that no matter how small or large one's sphere of influence may be, when one's life is concluded he will have left a great deal of generosity and tenderness behind.

DOROTHY FULDHEIM, AMERICAN LECTURER

A student is not better than his teacher. But when the student has fully learned all that he has been taught, then he will be like his teacher.

LUKE 6:40 ICB

By helping others you also help yourself. As these young people grow emotionally, physically and spiritually, so will you. There isn't any amount of money that can replace the pure self-satisfaction of knowing, that your love and your time have helped someone else.

HOWARD E. FERGUSON

Children should grow up seeing their parents on their knees before God, talking to Him.

DR. JAMES DOBSON

Beware! Some youngster is watching you. Be a good example for him.

ROBERT J. HALL

My life shall touch a dozen lives before this day is done,
Leave countless marks for good or ill ere sets the evening sun,

This is the wish I always wish, the prayer I always pray;
Lord, may my life help other lives it touches by the way.

UNKNOWN

Little Eyes Upon You

There are little eyes upon you and they're watching night
and day. There are little ears that quickly take in every word you
say. There are little hands all eager to do anything you do; And a
little boy who's dreaming of the day he'll be like you.

You're the little fellow's idol, you're the wisest of the wise.
In his little mind about you no suspicions ever rise. He believes
in you devoutly, holds all that you say and do; He will say
and do, in your way, when he's grown up like you.

There's a wide eyed little fellow who believes you're always
right; And his eyes are always opened, and he watched day and
night. You are setting an example every day in all you do, for the
little boy who's waiting to grow up to be like you.

UNKNOWN

"Johnny," the teacher asked, "what is the formula for water?"
"H, I, J, K, L, M, N, O," he replied. "That's not what I taught you."
"But you said the formula for water was H to O."

IDEAS FOR BETTER LIVING

FAMILY ROOTS GO DOWN AS YOU GROW UP

Direct your efforts to preparing youth for the path and less to preparing the path for the youth. The fortunate children are the ones who have everything money can't buy.

UNKNOWN

It takes wisdom to have a good family. It takes understanding to make it strong. It takes knowledge to fill a home with rare and beautiful treasures.

PROVERBS 24:3-4 ICB

When he was a crawler he left your feet to journey to the sofa and bring you a ball. When he was a toddler he left your side to journey across the grass and bring you a leaf. When he was a pre-school child he left your yard to journey next door and bring you back a neighbor's doll. Now he will journey into school and bring you back a piece of his new world...His journeys are all outward now, into that waiting world. But he feels the invisible and infinitely elastic threads that still guide him back to you. He returns to the base that is you, seeking rest and re-charging for each new leap into life.

PENELOPE LEACH, YOUR BABY AND CHILD

The roots of learning are bitter, but the fruit is sweet.

POLISH PROVERB

It is in the home that human relations put forth their first demands and develop their earliest patterns of response. It is in the home that decency or indecency is bred, and that fair play or foul becomes a rule of life. It is in the home that ambitions are developed and oriented—toward morally good or bad ends. It is in the home that genius is nurtured or perverted, and where average mentalities are given positive or negative direction.

UNKNOWN

A life-long blessing for children is to fill them with warm memories of times together. Happy memories become treasures in the heart to pull out on the tough days of adulthood.

CHARLOTTE DAVIS KASL, FINDING JOY

I see children as kites. You spend a lifetime trying to get them off the ground. You run with them until you're both breathless...they crash...you add a longer tail...Finally they are airborne, but they need more string so you keep letting it out. With each twist of the ball of twine there is a sadness that goes with the joy, because the kite becomes more distant, and somehow you know it won't be long before that beautiful creature will snap the lifeline that bound you together and soar as it was meant to soar—free and alone.

ERMA BOMBECK

There are two gifts we give our children
One is Roots...
the other is Wings.

UNKNOWN

AS YOU FLY AWAY—
REMEMBER YOUR ROOTS

The greatest gift you can give your children are the roots of
responsibility and the wings of independence.

DENIS WAITLY

To succeed, young people today should find work they like
to do and are interested in; they should learn how to get along
with people; they should try to develop and use common sense;
they should develop their imagination; they should be willing to
make changes. Finally, more important are these three qualities:
unselfishness in service to others, good personal habits and
strong faith in God. These things make for character.

J. WILLARD MARRIOTT

Watch your thoughts; they become words. Watch your words;
they become actions. Watch your actions; they become habits.
Watch your habits; they become character. Watch your character;
it becomes your destiny.

METROPOLITAN MILWAUKEE YMCA MOTTO

Train a child how to live the right way.
Then even when he is old, he will still live that way.

PROVERBS 22:6 ICB

Ten little two-letter words tell it all—
If it is to be, it is up to me.

UNKNOWN

The ultimate measure of man is not where he stands
in moments of comfort and convenience, but where he stands
at times of challenge and controversy.

MARTIN LUTHER KING, JR.

If we did all the things we are capable of doing,
we would literally astonish ourselves.

THOMAS EDISON

If a man does not keep pace with his companions, perhaps it is
because he hears a different drummer. Let him step to the music
which he hears, however measured or far away.

HENRY DAVID THOREAU

You've got to do your own growing
no matter how tall your grandfather was.

IRISH PROVERB

Take time to laugh. It is the music of the soul. Take time to think.
It is the source of power. Take time to play. It is the source of
perpetual youth. Take time to read. It is the fountain of wisdom.
Take time to pray. It is the greatest power on earth. Take time to be
friendly. It is the road to happiness. Take time to give. It is too short
a day to be selfish. Take time to work. It is the price of success.

UNKNOWN

Mid pleasures and palaces though we may roam,
Be it ever so humble there's no place like home...

JOHN HOWARD PAYNE

ACKNOWLEDGEMENTS

Scripture taken from the *Holy Bible, New International Version* ®. Copyright © 1973, 1978, 1984 by International Bible Society. Used by permission of Zondervan Publishing House. All rights reserved.

12,000 Religious Quotations, edited and compiled by Frank S. Mead. Reprinted 1989 by Baker Book House.

The Speaker's Sourcebook, by Eleanor Doan. Copyright ©1960 by Zondervan Publishing House, Grand Rapids, MI.

The International Dictionary of Thought, compiled by John P. Bradley, Leo F. Daniels, Thomas C. Jones. Copyright ©1969. Published by J. G. Ferguson Publishing Co., Chicago, IL.

Tough Times Never Last, but Tough People Do, Robert H. Schuller. Copyright ©1983. Permission granted by Crystal Cathedral Ministries. All rights reserved.

Wooden, John Wooden with Steve Jamison. Copyright ©1997. Published by Contemporary Books, an imprint of NTC/Contemporary Publishing Co., Lincolnwood, IL.

Encyclopedia of World Proverbs, compiled by Wolfgang Mieder. Copyright ©1986. Published by Prentice Hall, Englewood Cliffs, NJ.

Spirit of Leadership, complied by Fredrick C. Harrison. Copyright ©1989. Published by Leadership Education and Development, Inc., 1116 W. 7th St., Suite 175, Columbia, TN 38401.

The Ethics of Excellence. Copyright by Price Pritchett. Used by permission of Pritchett & Associates, Dallas, TX. All rights reserved.

Peter's Quotations, by Dr. Laurence J. Peters. A Bantam Book published by arrangement with William Morrow & Co.

Words To Live By, edited by William Nichols. Copyright ©1959. Published by Simon & Schuster, New York, NY.

Upwords Calendar, by Max Lucado. Copyright ©1994 by Word Publishing, Nashville, TN.

Wisdom for Men, by Bobb Biehl. Copyright ©1994. Published by LifeJourney Books, an imprint of Chariot Family Publishing.

The Best of Success, compiled by Wynn Davis. Published by Great Quotations, Inc., Aurora, IL.